INSIDE THE RAINBOW

of Love, Appreciation, Gratitude, Mindfulness Meditation, Spirituality and the Awakening Self

MUKTI LOVE

ISBN : 978-65-993818-9-8

Book Design by HMDpublishing

Acknowledgments

I dedicate this book to my earth mother, who first taught me freedom and love for the Great Mother, and who gave me wings to fly far, beyond, and into all directions. I am deeply grateful.

Thank you to all mothers and children of the Earth who give me hope for a loving world. I am deeply grateful to all masters, teachers, bodhisattvas, angels, brothers and sisters of the heart who supported this journey and made this book come to life. Special thanks to David Arrufat, who continuously teaches me about freedom and love for Our Mother; to Valerie Cervantes and to Johanna Craven for the time, encouragement and love dedicated to helping this birth.

I am deeply grateful for the rainbow.

I embrace this moment with flowers, smiles, tears, and a warm hug from my heart.

CONTENTS

PREFACE

There was a time I was wild. As a tandem paragliding pilot in Nepal, by the feet of the Himalayas, my job was to take people flying with me. For eleven years I lived in a stone hut without electricity, bathing in the rivers, in awe of our mother's beauty, and literally flying high between the clouds most of my days.

After many years of psychology studies and living in big cities in Brazil and the US, I had totally broken up with civilization. This path took me into meditation, prayer and the curiosity of a rich and exciting inner world I was about to discover. I was learning to fly with different wings – the wings of dreams. I was in search of freedom, of course, but this path took to me into another dimension: inner freedom.

Later, destiny took me from Nepal to an island in the Philippines, where I got in touch with ancient shamanism adapted to the new days, uplifted by the power of music and sounds. I ended up living in a raw food community, in a detox and spiritual retreat center, and I immersed myself in sound healing and meditation for nearly three years. From there, I went to Switzerland to build a place of healing with the help of many volunteers, holding space and hosting beautiful people from all over the world.

I knew I was giving birth to a book, and I was responsible for bringing it into the world and raising it. My book would have its own life someday, it could never belong to me, just like a child. I was just a channel or a kind of portal for it to materialize and pass through. I knew nothing really belonged to me or to anyone on this Earth, and since we are all just passengers, we take nothing with us except the experiences we have lived and shared. We just nurture the creative process that life is.

I have a friend who is a composer, and she told me that when she is creating music she feels as though the song already exists and is just coming out of her. The same is true for the writing of this book. I had to translate and express it in words that people could understand and relate to. I was on an airplane, traveling home from Brazil, when I had the feeling I was pregnant. Not with a child, but with a book, as it was already alive and in existence within me in such a way that it had to come out. So, the life of this book is the same as the life of a child; it does not belong to me or anyone, but to all life.

This work began through audios I recorded during peaceful walks through the forests while I was living in Switzerland. Even though it is written in English, it is the language of the heart, which is not limited to any spoken language. Just feel this truth, and share your love with more and more people around you. Let us spread seeds of love and compassion everywhere! This is the nature of this book. It is time to bring it into action, and to transform everything that needs to be transformed.

On these pages, we will explore inner gardening: consciously cultivating and planting seeds inside ourselves. For me, life is like a garden, and we have all the seeds inside of us. The seeds that will grow are the ones we nourish and water every day. I will share my personal practice of inner gardening and some amazing abundant seeds to harvest in life. I will also present the scientific background to what I am discussing.

After twenty years of studying the secrets of the mind and putting them into practice, I can say that I speak from experience as a psychologist and a scientist, not only as a dreamer and adventurer. I love uniting science and spirituality and do not believe in separation and segregation. I do believe in our uniqueness, but I choose to see that we all come from the same source and live on this same spaceship called Earth. We are all cells of the same giant body of the Universe. With a good sense of humor, science marries with spirituality to form a beautiful relationship!

For me, life is about sharing – and so is love. It makes me so happy to share everything with you: ancient teachings, science, visions, and insights, combined with the most practical, simple and powerful meditations. Profound tools to build and support a New Earth energy based in gratitude, love and forgiveness.

As much as I want to heal myself, I also want humanity to heal from all ignorance, pain and suffering. I know I am not the only one to feel this. I am speaking on behalf of many because, deep inside, love is really the essence of every human being. I know that we, as a collective, will get there. We will find our way. Earth will be a planet full of love one day! I am not the only one dreaming of this or working on it. There are many people awakening; many angels living through love.

I am aware that we are not separate. We are part of one reality, one organism. We have a collective unconscious mind and a supreme life force within us. We are not born with a manual to follow, and it takes many years to master the complexity and the simplicity of our existence. This book is the result of a life of experience on the way to freedom and liberation.

We are gifted with a wonderful planet to live on, with its sacred waters, rays of sunlight, forests, oceans and mountains. The air we breathe is such an amazing, precious gift. But are we allowing ourselves to experience it fully? Are we allowing ourselves to live the best version of our most incredible dreams, to experience who we truly are?

These questions have followed me for so long and somehow beautiful insights and experiences came through me. I am about to share all with you, with my heart open and full of love. My only wish is to get older and grow, flourish and give fruits to share and spread good seeds everywhere. This is an invitation for you to join in this light work of inner gardening – let's spread seeds!

For as long as I can remember, my connection to nature has been a relationship of love. The sky and the stars, the oceans and the mountains, the forests and the lakes, they love me and I love them. We are in love and we are one. In my oldest childhood memories, I can hear nature speaking to me, and I know Earth is and always will be my mother. No matter which part of the world I lived in, home was more of a sacred place inside of me. Yes, the mother is inside me, and everything else too. I am eternally grateful for our mother Earth, who provides us with a sustainable life. Infinite gratitude is the word.

This book is addressed to all dreamers and nature lovers, especially the lovers of life. I offer you this work with humbleness, hoping it will touch your heart as much as it has touched mine. I offer it not only to myself and to you, but to all living beings and creatures from our past, present and future generations. I offer and I bow in gratitude, knowing that everything we do is not only for ourselves but for all life on Earth. Given the interdependence of life, when we heal ourselves, we are also healing our entire planet. With your permission, we will go into this journey to dream together, to bring healing and transformation to our lives and to the whole planet. We can have everything we deserve for our highest self because this is our birthright. We claim our birthright now.

Are you ready? Let's fly high with the wings of the dreams! Open your wings to the freedom of your soul and enjoy the journey!

INTRODUCTION

The Alchemist of Love

"What is essential is invisible to the eyes," said the voice. *A voice? Whose voice is this? Is it mine? Or is it consciousness passing through me?* Without pause, the voice continued, "The alchemist is the one who turns EVERYTHING into LOVE."

The sentence resonated inside of me for a long time, like an echo. Then silence. Deep silence and one long breath. I recognized life in me through this breath. The last word, LOVE, was resonating deeply, and suddenly I could hear everything around me. I could hear the wind, the crickets, my breath, and the voice whispering. It was powerful. Just a whisper in my ears, passing through my mind and somehow translating into a message received by my heart.

Somehow I knew these were two important sentences that I must never forget. I repeated to myself, “What is essential is invisible to the eyes...” I recognized that sentence from the book of Saint-Exupery, *The Little Prince*. It was full of wisdom. The second sentence, I wasn’t too sure about... I repeated once again, “The alchemist is the one who turns EVERYTHING into LOVE.” *Wow! Is that possible?* I thought to myself. I felt I had to go deeper into its meaning to fully understand it.

The first sentence was quite easy for me. I had been working hard on letting go of the habit of seeing things just in their physical aspect and instead regarding them as energy, frequency and vibration. I was specifically working with the energy of gratitude, love and forgiveness – things that were extremely essential to me. But the second sentence triggered me; I had to reflect more on that. Could I – or anyone – become such an alchemist? To transform EVERYTHING into LOVE? Would that really be possible?!

At that point, I had to close my eyes, keep breathing and feel the deepness of my heart. And so I am inviting you now, please, close your eyes just for a second and take one deep breath with me. Let’s take a few deep breaths together. Visualize and feel the beauty of our Earth, and recognize that same beauty in your heart. You are beautiful; you are amazing; you are a sparkle of light. You are the reflection of the beauty you see around and inside of you.

I could not help but smile to myself, feeling compassion for myself all the times I had forgotten my own beauty and for all human beings who had forgotten it too. Who was really smiling? Was it me? Or was it the consciousness inside of me? Who was truly breathing? I was curious to know the truth.

If there was one thing I knew through my own experiences it was that by practicing this kind of breath, our lives start shining with bright and vibrant colors. When I was in my twenties, colorful, successive rainbows started showing up, and since then I have had a long-lasting relationship with rainbows. You might wonder, *How could someone have a relationship with rainbows? You must be kidding!* However, I assure you, it is possible. I will explain this in detail later in the book.

It seems that everything is possible in this Universe when you access the realm of dreams. First, are you in a dream or are you in a reality? What is reality for you? Everything that was ever created in this world came from a strong dream of someone, and then their focus and work brought it to life. We dreamed of airplanes, technology, music, poetry, but we also created sufferings, bombs and war. We have the potential to dream about anything, and the dreams we focus on manifest and become reality. The Universe works with us in its creation.

Can you imagine how nice it would be if there were signs on the road that said, *Pay attention to your dreams, please!*? It would remind us how important it is to dream. Now, ask yourself, what kind of dreams are you having? Are your dreams only for yourself, such as desires for material and physical things? Or are they expanded for the greater good of others too, including human beings and nature? Who is the dreamer and who is awakening?

What I call dreams are beyond thoughts and intentions. Dreams are an infinite ocean of creativity, possibilities, heart, soul and hope. There are mysterious, beautiful messages in the form of dreams. No nightmares. My intention is to share amazing spiritual insights with you so that we can transform our realities. We can begin to live our dreams and open ourselves up to a collective awakening that is already happening.

So many people's dreams are limited to their wealth and possessions, in other words, desires. Others can't dare to dream and live in an awakened state, so they dream only during their sleep. Maybe they are too shy or depressed, or maybe they are not exactly sure how to create or experience their dreams. Many of us have forgotten how to dream because we have made ourselves way too busy and logical. So I wonder: why would most of us dream only about having material things, like cars, houses, pleasures, or a lot of money in our bank account? What are the limits to our dreams? We don't need to dream only for ourselves, do we?

There are no limits to our dreams – everything is possible in the realm of dreams. Why should we remain selfish and narrow-minded, afraid to dream about the happiness of humankind and of all living beings and creatures? Real happiness comes from relationships, love, kindness, and prosperity both for ourselves and for everyone in this world. Dreaming about the expansion of our minds allows us to experience life to the fullest, sharing in our richness and finding peace, love and compassion for ourselves and for all.

Can we dream of a world with no war, no competition, no violence, misery or children dying of hunger? Above all, we should not be afraid to dream beyond ourselves. I have been dreaming for Mother Earth, for a collective consciousness to expand, for the sprouts of loving seeds to grow everywhere on our planet. This energy can heal us all, and I hope I'm not the only one – like in John Lennon's song, "Imagine."

I want to share all my experiences about dreaming, awakening, inner gardening, and cultivating seeds. I believe we are here on this planet to heal and uplift each other. We are here to rise together! Why would anyone wish to rise alone? I want to rise together with you, in a collective awakening. Let us take this ascent!

I want to share with dreamers and non-dreamers alike. I want to support the dream of the rainbow, and help bring more beauty into our lives.

We can breathe and dream together for our whole planet!

I know I have the Universe inside of me; I know that I am the Universe. And so are you. I allow myself to dream beyond myself, and to spread loving seeds everywhere. This is an invitation for you to join me in this mission. Remember: by healing ourselves, we will heal our entire planet.

I know sometimes it is hard to be enthusiastic in a world full of pain and misery, but let's call on the beauty that exists around us. Let's ask the help of the flowers, the blue sky, the little birds, and of all the angels and masters to support us in our most difficult moments. Everything is transforming and we too can transform ourselves, our experiences and emotions. We can heal.

MISSION

We have no time to lose. Life is short.

Have you ever thought about your mission on this Earth? What do you truly love? Why are you here? What is your dream?

What you focus on in your mind is what you create and experience in your life. Only your heart knows the answer. Dive deep into your heart and start doing what you truly love now. Do not be afraid and your dreams will start to happen. It does not matter how old you are, you can always change for the better and learn. It is never too late to plant healthy seeds. These seeds will continue to grow even after we leave this planet. Start planting now and let's make a better and beautiful future together. Wouldn't it be amazing to become such an alchemist, to tap into the magic of the Universe and turn EVERYTHING into LOVE? Could it really be possible? Could we transform even bad and negative thoughts, emotions and experiences into LOVE?

"Yes! Everything is possible in this Universe! You can learn if you wish," the inner voice was still whispering... "The moment you start, the magic in you will be unleashed, as it is already happening at this very moment. Yes, you can become such an alchemist."

However, in other parts of my mind, questions were piling up: *Is there anything that is NOT possible in this world? Are we limited or unlimited by our imagination and our dreams?*

I couldn't help but repeat the words, to make sure I did not forget: "It is already happening at this very moment... And you are on your way to becoming such an alchemist, to turn EVERYTHING into LOVE."

Wow, how inspiring! What a beautiful dream!

You must go for it, and do all that you love. For how much longer will you wait? There is no time to lose. You can start dreaming and loving now!

If you have arrived here, then this is the right story for you; the right time, and the right place. The information contained in this book might be exactly what you need at this moment. Maybe you feel you have had enough suffering in your life, in your past, or around you. Maybe your soul feels like you have had enough, and it is time to change.

I believe there is an individual and collective awakening happening on our planet, and that is why we are here. The Universe wants us to experience true LOVE. The Universe loves us! We are ready to graduate, to go to another level of understanding, by going forward on a spiritual (r) evolution.

Life is a gift, and so is this present moment. We have received many gifts from the Universe! I am your gift and you are mine. Being able to write and read is also a gift. We give each other the present moment, we dream and we awaken together.

I ask you: Are you a dreamer? Who is this dreamer? Is there anything that can define you? Do you want to dream and fly like a free spirit? Do you want to remember how to dream again? We should never underestimate the power of dreams, nor the power of a single atom. Are you afraid to dream, or are you ready to experience the most beautiful dreams in your life? No matter what your answers are, this road will show us the way. With my deep love for the Universe, I say, please, use me to spread your LOVE. Whatever love means to you, we will dive into the heart and find out.

Life is the biggest adventure and the biggest mystery at the same time. You can laugh about it if you feel too overwhelmed by the infinitude of the Universe and of these words. Actually, everything that makes you laugh and smile from your heart is the best medicine you can find in this world. So yes, please, laugh! We can enjoy life when we allow ourselves to be playful like the little children we once were. For many of us, growing up meant forgetting about our inner child. Or perhaps, even worse, we never actually had the chance to know or love and care for him/her enough. The sparkle of life that can so easily be seen in children's eyes has been dimmed or diluted entirely in our adult eyes.

In our awakening process, we return to our inner child who is free of judgment, concepts, and theories. Only then we can learn to embrace life again. We can let it all go and transform. Yes, it is possible. We can transform even our pain into LOVE.

Everything is possible in this Universe!

Feeling at Home

The day I decided to start writing this manuscript, I found myself glancing out of a little window in my Swiss home. It was a 350-year-old wooden chalet at the edge of a small, peaceful old village, which has witnessed little change in the last half a millennium. I was watching a flurry of snow fall outside. Within my view was a far-reaching, tranquil lake encased by a gargantuan wall of glistening white mountains. The pristine nature around me had this unfathomable power; words are just not enough to describe its magnificence. Truly, this landscape can lure you into a hypnotic trance, preventing you from breaking away from its grasp. There is something magical about this part of the world.

I often wonder how I found myself calling Switzerland home. It had been over three years since I started the project of building a place of healing, meditation and retreats there. I called it the Energy School and it was born from my rainbow dreams. It was a precious and safe place, but my true home was always inside of me. Home was a unified body, mind and soul, and I practiced being in the here and now, as much as I could.

I have always been something of a nomad. It had been almost 20 years since I'd left my birth country of Brazil in search of adventure, and to explore the world. After many years of scientific studies, I wanted to be free of all theories and to actually experience life. I was not afraid to dream big and to go very far, so I went traveling through India. I started my first job adventure while traveling. I created my own online travel agency and became a pilgrims' tour guide in India and Nepal, taking yoga groups into monasteries, holy places and the sacred Himalayan mountains – my favorite destinations. I found my spirit gravitating towards those eastern regions; India and Nepal, and later Thailand, Indonesia and the Philippines.

Although I have lived both in the wild and in populous cities, I have never truly been part of the so-called "system." For as long as I can remember, I have had a desire to be within nature and become more intimate with the elemental forces of this planet. I seemed to feel happier the further away I was from civilization. My heart guided me to a stone hut by a riverbank in Nepal, next to Phewa Lake by the feet of the Himalayas. I ended up living there for 11 years. It was a deep, intimate experience with nature, living with Mother Earth and developing a relationship with the Mother.

In Nepal, I had no TV, no telephone and, for more than seven years, not even a computer. On rare occasions I would travel into town to check my email. This lifestyle made me feel as if I had traversed through some kind of gap in space and time, going back hundreds of years into the past. For most, these circumstances would be a great inconvenience, but for me it was a choice. I had experienced life in the rat race, or the "real world" as most people put it, and it was not something I found particularly attractive. I preferred to live on another frequency, unrestricted by the illusions and arbitrary expectations that society places upon us. I just wanted to be with nature, with Mother Earth.

After living for such a long time in a remote home with no electricity, I fully embraced minimalism and the serene peace that only the simplicity of nature can provide. I had the privilege of bathing in the rivers every day, soaring through the Himalayas, embarking on paragliding expeditions across untouched parts of the world, and what started out as an old hobby became my new job.

My passion for flying made me fall in love with Nepal. There, I also met and fell in love with my life partner, my dear Deva Hanuman, "The Flying God." I felt at home! He had just started a paragliding school, where I also worked as a paragliding tandem pilot, taking passengers on breath-taking journeys across the beautiful Himalayas. That was my job; to fly and take passengers with me on my wings!

I would fly through and above the clouds and the mountain ranges around Pokhara, and land beside the gorgeous Phewa Lake. People from all over the world would join me to experience the dream of flying. I shared with them my passion and my love for the sky. The sky and I had a deep, intimate relationship. And I spent most of my days loving and living in its immense beauty.

A few years passed and a big earthquake hit. Many political problems in Nepal followed. We decided to leave, moving to a tiny island in the Philippines, with the most beautiful sunsets I have ever witnessed. Every day was a spectacular healing with the sun and the ocean. Tears of joy and gratitude would run down my face, either from meditation, from walking on the beach, the miracle of walking on Earth, or even kitesurfing, which had become my new passion. I was in love with the blue ocean, and many times, as I rode the wind and the sea, I would say internally, "Thank you, Mother Earth, for allowing me to experience your beauty in so many ways! I love you."

I was ready to go even deeper into the heart. In the Philippines, I made so many beautiful new friends and I deepened my yoga practice. I felt a creative process was taking place among the white mountains and the blue sea. I started sharing my meditation practices with groups of people, opening my heart fully, and offering sessions with the Tibetan singing bowls I had brought all the way from Nepal. It was mostly volunteer and non-profit work.

After a year, as our finances dwindled, we moved to Palawan; to a small bamboo hut next to a raw food community and retreat space called Bahay Kalipay, commonly known as "the house of happiness." There, I shared love through meditation and sound healing with more and more people. I met so many beautiful souls that, to me, seemed like angels on Earth. Freedom had taken on another perspective. I had surrendered to the Universe and became an awakened dreamer, opening and touching my own heart to find out who I truly was.

My time in the Philippines was magical. I fully embraced minimalism again, almost living as a hermit. I shared the smallest bamboo hut I had ever been with my children, now two and six years old; Joy, born in Thailand and Iara, in Nepal. In spite of all challenges, we always managed well. While their father was still trying to work in Nepal, we enjoyed life in the Philippines. My possessions were almost nothing, only the Tibetan singing bowls. My diet was mainly raw food, fresh fruits and coconuts. Yoga and healing were my daily practices. I had never felt so rich from inside. In the simplicity of a bamboo hut, the children were so happy, playing on the beach most of the days. The only luxury I had was a lovely babysitter who helped me during parts of the day so I could devote time to yoga, healing practices and being in the community.

Three years later, we decided to go to Switzerland for both our children's education and greater job opportunities. It was a big decision to return to civilization and to enter the system. We found an old and amazing Swiss chalet to live in, and there I started building a new retreat space with the help of many volunteers. My only wish was that I could experience and create heaven wherever I was. Even though we had little money, the Universe had proven once again that everything is possible with the power of Love. We are not limited by any obstacles when we trust this power. Everything is always provided.

In short, all these magical stories deserve a second book; this is but a glimpse of them. This book is focused on inner gardening and planting seeds to activate the power inside ourselves. It is never too late for inner gardening. The Earth is here to help us, as is the sun, the water, and all the seeds. This is the beauty of inner gardening. The work is done to create a better future, to nourish ourselves, to experience our inner heaven. This is simply what happens when we cultivate these seeds. Feeling and nurturing it inside ourselves, we can all become alchemists and transform everything into Love.

All we need is to start cultivating the fertile soil of our minds, to observe the nature of it as we activate the power source. We allow the Earth to help us as we inspire and support one another!

Smile! The time has arrived and it is NOW! It is not in the future. It is only NOW that exists, and in that moment, we create our future.

It Is Time

A Healing Mantra

> *"Our body and mind are sustained by the cosmos. The clouds in the sky nourish us; the light of the sun nourishes us. The cosmos offers us vitality and love in every moment. Despite this fact, some people feel isolated and alienated from the world. By our practice, we can approach such a person, and we can open the door of his or her heart to the world and to the love and magic that is always happening: 'Dear one, I know you are suffering a lot. I am here for you, just as the trees and the flowers are here for you.' The suffering is there, but something else is there: the miracle of life. With this mantra, you will help everyone to realize this and open the door of their closed heart."*
>
> *Thich Nhat Hanh*

Time has finally arrived for you, for us, and for all of humanity to be happy and free! Our happiness and freedom start individually. First inside ourselves, then outwards to the external world. Only after our personal transformation can they fully expand into all directions.

After a long journey of the soul, so many experiences and sufferings, we are finally ready! We do not need to suffer anymore. We can consciously become alchemists to transform our pain and suffering into love – and this is when the rainbow shows up in our lives, representing the beauty and the wonders of life.

We will feel inside what is most sacred in us. We start to see our body as a temple, our words as a sacred voice, and everything around us as sacred. This divine energy that we decided to call God (or whatever name you choose to call this energy) is in everything and everywhere. It can take so many forms. Divine energy is coming to me, to you and to everyone who activates the power that has always been there inside of us. It is the power of nature. It is when we remember who we truly are.

A book is made up of words, but it goes far beyond words. A person is made of flesh and blood, but goes far beyond that. In the end, what really matters is the love that we create in our lives, and in all we do. My mission here is to pass that love on and to keep it alive. I am only passing on the light, the colors, and the seeds of beauty that I have been experiencing in this lifetime. I chose beauty, and I will share this vision with you from a life full of dreams. It never really belonged to me to begin with, but to all of us. In truth, everything belongs to Mother Earth.

Yes, experiences, wonders and dreams were grown inside me, but now have a life themselves and are asking to be shared. Writing this book felt like a pregnancy, giving birth to another form of life. A natural birth made out of love with this divine energy and the miracle of life.

This energy has always been there and it will always be; it was just waiting to be seen, to be spoken to, and to be loved. I love the mystery of life and I hope you will love it too. I hope more alchemists are being born every day, transforming everything into love. This is the power of the dream we can generate together, and it will be so strong that we will heal ourselves and our beloved Earth.

"May all beings be happy and free."

Sanskrit mantra: Lokah Samastah Sukhino Bhavantu

Now, I would like first to share with you the seeds. We must iron out the kinks within our soul and open ourselves up with humility. As we bring light into our inner world, we are able to see things more clearly. Only then can we bring light and provide more value to our lives. Meditation is the catalyst for our true self to manifest. It is like planting seeds, watering them and exposing them to the light.

Let's start planting seeds!

PART I

INNER GARDENING & SEEDS

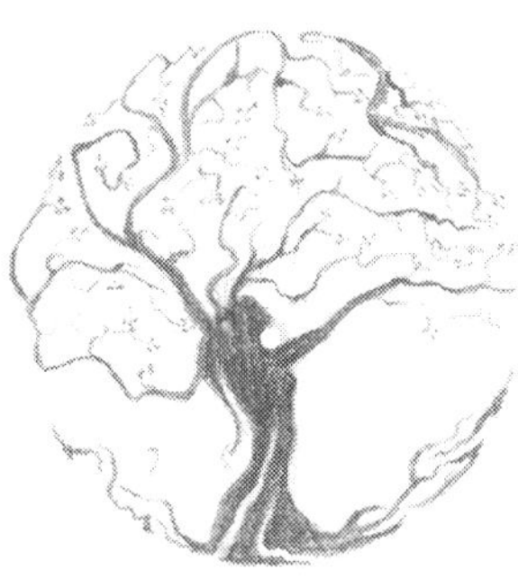

1.
INNER GARDEN

My aim is to plant seeds of love, compassion, forgiveness, joy and happiness in my life, my surroundings, and everywhere I go. I believe we all want to have a joyful life. Freedom and happiness are our birth right. So let's go down the path to happiness!

I saw my notion of happiness change and expand in the same way the entire Universe changes and expands. We can't buy joy and happiness in a store—we can only cultivate it, and it starts in the inner gardens of the mind, heart and spirit. We can nurture and water the many seeds inside of ourselves.

Love and compassion are some of the best seeds a human being can plant and harvest, and those who nurture it become a blessing for those who are around them, and for the entire planet. Love is expanding, transforming and unfolding continuously like everything else. I understand this as a sort of "inner garden": the mind is the soil to take care of, and with the heart, a place we can cultivate the good seeds, let them grow, and bear fruits. Choose the seeds you want to grow, offer those seeds to the good soil of your mind, let the sunshine come in, water them and you will see how they bloom. It follows the same process as nature. We have all seeds within us; we decide which ones we are going to water. Anyone can cultivate their mind's soil with nutrients, which are nothing but good thoughts. Literally, soil needs water and sunlight, so drink water from pure sources and bask in the sunlight. After almost 20 years of cultivating beautiful seeds, taking loving care and watering them, I can taste the fruits, the bliss, and the sweetness of love.

Nature is asking me to share. Nature is asking me to let go of what's left of my ego. To expose my inner world and all of the craziness, vulnerability, and intimacy that comes with it. I am doing it out of love, and with not a single doubt. I am listening to my heart, as it wants to communicate and spread those seeds and help others with their inner gardening processes and dreams.

Inner gardening is planting and watering seeds inside ourselves. We give our mind the right soil, by allowing the right thoughts and feelings. We clean and prepare the soil by cleaning ourselves on the inside; taking out the rocks and weeds, observing and taking care of our thoughts. It means taking care and watering our seeds, tending to our inner garden, nurturing it, and letting the sunshine do its work. Nature will help the seeds grow beautiful and strong, and at the right time, we will harvest what we have planted. When we cultivate good seeds in ourselves, we will have many beautiful, delicious fruits in our inner garden.

2.
SEEDS OF LOVE

INVESTING IN LIFE

The most important thing we can have is love. Anything done without love is a waste of precious life. Investing in life is all about love, but it is also about time. It is so true what Buddha once said: our biggest illusion is that we think we have time. I came to understand that I have to make my decisions based on love in the present moment. We tend to reserve happiness for the future, but in reality there is no future. Decisions have to be made now. We must choose our own love and happiness, taking responsibility for our decisions and actions. Now.

From the moment I came to understand this, I would do everything with love or I wouldn't do it at all. Doing everything with love became my fundamental philosophy. This was also a time when I was singing a lot of the Sanskrit mantra *Baba Nam Kevalam*, which means "all is love" or "love is everywhere and everything." I could spend many hours singing this mantra.

Love is the most precious seed human beings can experience.

I committed to basing my decisions on love, through the eyes of compassion and in the direction of what I loved. It was not a complicated thing to do—very much the opposite. It was a pleasant, simple, and genuine philosophy to follow. By doing everything with love, all choices became easier. In the eyes of some, maybe it was not a very realistic way to live, but it was not a decision from the mind—it came from my heart. I did not care about religions, only about love.

I was allowing my heart to guide my life, with the help of my mind and all thoughts that stemmed from it. My mind understood and agreed, and my mind was also happy to be following the heart. The results proved to me that listening to the heart was always the best choice. My mind was no longer in control; instead the mind was honoring the heart, with humbleness, and a focused intention on love.

Neither my ideas nor my feelings were my identity. I knew the mind was there for me, somehow a part of me, but it was not me. Even my feelings were not me. My feelings were like the ocean's waves, a reflection of all the conditioning I was exposed to. Feelings were only the waves, not the ocean. I could speak to myself, to my mind and to my feelings. Somehow, I understood that there was a consciousness behind it all.

I did not fully understand how it worked, but I knew the mind was limited to the programs we run inside ourselves. With some knowledge, I learned it was possible to reset, clean, install and run new programs inside the mind. For this reason, I am sharing, through this book, some of these programs and showing that it is possible for anyone to access this power. And to go deep inside the heart.

Not long ago, someone asked me, "But how can I listen to my heart?" This is a question many of us have, and this is mainly what I am writing about—how to listen to the heart. This question is something our society is suffering from, but I am not here to point out our problems. My choice is to be less critical, complaining and labelling will not give us the solutions we need.

We want practical, easy and intelligent solutions, and inner gardening may be the solution we have been looking for; planting and cultivating seeds in our garden of life. Every seed we plant will grow.

Every thought we have is like a seed, and every time we feel and think something we water it.

Only when we activate the love, the heart space inside ourselves, will we be able to upgrade to a new level of consciousness and understanding, and transform our lives for the better. If the heart space is not activated, the energy is blocked, no matter how many doctors we see or how much medication we take. We must open the heart. The energy must flow inside ourselves, for in doing this we cultivate seeds of love and compassion. By doing so, the energy circulates and liberates us from all ignorance, negativity and blockages that cause us illness, pain and suffering. Love can heal.

In other words, listening to our heart is learning to love. Certainly, love is the answer and the solution for everything. Love is the answer to what we have always been looking for, and it is right inside of us. It is never too late to cultivate these seeds.

What makes you happy? What do you love? Go to the truth of your soul. Feel it. Think about it. You can start by writing it down. What are you waiting for?

There was a time that my answer to these questions was something like: I want to feel free; to travel; to live in pure nature; to let go; to live a simple life; to fly with my paragliding wings above the clouds; to contribute to creating a better life on the planet. I had realized that I could not be happy living in a big city, driving a car in traffic jams, living in a concrete building, or leading any kind of artificial life. I did not want that anymore, and I would not force myself into it, which meant I had to change my lifestyle completely. I did not know how I was going to do that, but I felt a strong need for personal freedom.

I understood that to change my lifestyle, I needed courage and trust. We need to be bold enough to go into the unknown, trusting that the Universe always provides everything we need. So, with that wisdom in my heart, I prepared to move away from the big city and all its problems. Rio de Janeiro, in Brazil, is a very beautiful city. But even though I was living close to the forest and the ocean, the city remained very polluted and violent, and was home to more than 13 million people. The density and the moral values of the population did not attract me. Instead, I wanted to travel and discover the world. Despite my young age, I had enough courage to go on my own. I finished my studies, prepared my departure, said good-by to my boyfriend who had no audacity to join this adventure, and left with all the little savings I had. I did not know how long they would last. But I knew that this was my path, that I was the one choosing my experiences and, thus, creating my own reality.

I went wild, back to my origins. I wanted to return to nature, and to feel and live with Mother Earth. I would not allow my fears to stop me. My love and trust in the Universe was much bigger, and I didn't want a small adventure—I wanted a big one! I wanted to go as far as I could and see as much as I could. So I threw myself to the unknown, trusting the divine force that gives life and constantly supports us.

Understanding Love and Connectedness

One day, a friend of mine, full of emotion, asked, "Why is Love so painful?" This was a loaded question, and although it is common for people to regard love and romance as synonyms, we need to understand that love is something much bigger than two people. Love, actually, refers to the connection between all living beings and creatures, and therefore, also includes romantic relationships. However, love is not directed only to a person, but rather it embraces that person and everything else in life as it expands.

On the other hand, it is true that both love and pain exist. Indeed, life contains suffering and joy; they cannot exist separately on our planet. It is up to us to choose what we experience.

Do you want to experience suffering, or do you want to experience the wonders of life? What lifestyle are you choosing in order to live your experiences? Which seeds have you been planting in the fertile soil of your mind?

We are not victims of the life we create but quite the opposite. We are responsible for it, and this is why we really need to forgive ourselves. We forgive our mistakes, our judgments, we forgive the past—

and in doing so we set ourselves free. Only then we can create the life we choose because we have become free of all that old stuff we were carrying.

Forgiveness starts within ourselves and our families, and includes forgiveness even for all we do not understand. This is one of the most important practices. Even if I forget at times, I will forgive myself again, for all the times I had forgotten. Forgive your mistakes and be humble enough to recognize that no one is perfect. We are not victims, not even from our past. Do not put yourself in this position because when you do you become paralyzed. When you take responsibility for your choices and actions, only then will you be able to learn, transform, and experience something different in your life. Only when you step out of the victim role will you take responsibility for the life you are living.

So, going back to my friend's question; yes, if love becomes limited to one or to a small group of people, one can suffer. Selfish love happens only when ego is present. Selfish love causes us to get caught in an illusion of separation. On the other hand, expanded love comes from within and projects outwardly to all living beings and creatures. It is when this energy fully opens our hearts that this feeling of unity grows, and we become conscious of how we are all connected and part of an integrated system.

There is no real separation between us and all the life around us. Separated or isolated, we simply couldn't exist. When we understand that we are part of this creation—*Paramapurusha*, the Sanskrit word for "the creator and creature"—we accept our non-separated existence, our wholeness with everything else.

Everything is contained inside us. Trees, animals, the ocean and the sky are within us. Without them we cannot exist because our existence is made of non-self elements. Put simply, a separated self does not exist. You can't just identify yourself with a name and think you are a separate person. This is really an illusion of the ego, which is nothing but the ignorance of the limited mind. Only by going deeper into the present moment can you shed your ego and realize who you truly are.

You are the result and the combination of everything that exists. Your own personal lineage and the entire planet are inside of you. We are part of the infinite love and creativity of the Universe; of this amazing, beautiful, and incredible life. This is the inner power that we can connect with at any time. This is our true home. This understanding expands our vision and we can no longer identify with our suffering. It simply dissolves away as we understand we are something much bigger than we could have ever imagined.

Every human needs love from the moment of their conception. It is our most essential need. Love is the most powerful energy that exists. Love can transform everything. This is the essence of all teachings.

All masters of love do not teach religion but just one thing: for you to become a master of yourself. Real masters are not the ones who have more students or disciples, but the ones who create more masters of love. We all have the potential to become masters of ourselves.

Relationships

A Harvard research study by psychiatrist Robert Waldinger, the longest ever conducted, tracked the lives of 724 men for an entire lifetime in order to determine what kept them happy and healthy throughout life. Year after year, the study followed these men, their work, their home lives, and their health, all the while not knowing how their life stories would turn out. The project followed them since they were teenagers in 1938. The group consisted of men from various economic and social backgrounds, from Boston's poorest neighborhoods to Harvard undergrads (president John F. Kennedy was even part of the original group).

Over the years, the researchers collected all kinds of health information, and every two years they asked members questions about their lives and their mental and emotional wellness. They even interviewed family members. Specific questionnaires were used in the scientific research to assess happiness levels. Even though measuring happiness is neither simple nor easy, the researchers found that specific traits and behaviors were linked with increased levels of happiness across the entire group. The results proved that happiness has nothing to do with wealth or success. The clearest message to emerge from the study was:

Good relationships keep us happier and healthier.

Loneliness kills. It decreases brain function, resulting in a shortened life. But one can be lonely in a crowd, or even lonely in a marriage. The second biggest finding of Waldinger's research was that the number of friends a person has does not matter—it's the quality of those close relationships that actually matters. Although living in high-conflict relationships is extremely bad for our health, warm and happy relationships are very good for our health. According to Dr. Waldinger, the healthiest men in their 80s were the ones who were most satisfied with their relationships at age 50.

We humans are social beings. Ultimately, we like to be with others, to have a family or a community, share our lives, and feel loved. We want to make genuine connections in all our relationships and share happy moments in a blissful environment. When there is an absence of connection with others, we may feel lonely and empty inside. No matter how much money one might have, the ultimate goal is love and connection—and those things cannot be purchased, but must be cultivated within. Many people struggle in their relationships because they don't take enough care of themselves. They don't cultivate their inner garden, and are unable to recognize the tremendous value of doing so.

When we create healthy and beautiful relationships, we truly value them. Remember, it is never too late to form beautiful relationships. We can be aware of all the relationships we create, and learn to be selective of them. We can form strong relations in our heart; we can be pure and authentic.

In order to establish beautiful relationships with others, we must first value and establish a beautiful relationship with ourselves. If we are not genuinely valuing ourselves, who will?

When you arrive at the point of loving and valuing yourself—by respecting, being completely honest, gentle and kind to yourself, nourishing those beautiful seeds in you—then you will recognize how you are being treated as you deserve to be. It happens by giving your body, mind and spirit the right nourishment, such as good amounts of exercise and rest, feeding yourself with life force energy, empowering beautiful thoughts in your mind, taking time for your soul in nature, experiencing times of silence, peace and calmness, as well as enthusiasm, laughter and joy. By loving yourself, you will clearly see if someone is not valuing you enough or putting you down, and so can choose not to continue wasting your time with them. You have the right to walk away, to let him or her go, yet still find compassion for that person. Do not waste time; walk in the direction of those who value you as much as you value yourself, and those who can love themselves too. Remember, if you do not love and value yourself, nobody else will. Loving ourselves is the first step in creating beautiful relationships. Protect the beauty you hold inside. You are precious, you are beautiful!

Beauty is a combination of our inner and outer world. Beauty is a person that is pure, with genuine, innocent and honest thoughts in mind; a person with an open, compassionate and kind heart. Take in this beautiful energy and use it to nourish a beautiful relationship; it might be with your partner, a friend, a family member, a co-worker, etc. Healthy relationships are built when we recognize the value of the people around us. Bring them peace by transmitting your inner peace. Peace is the foundation of love. Always have in mind: peace is not something outside of yourself. Only when we return to our inner peace can we can experience true love in our relationships and with the entire planet. Peace and understanding is the ground on which love can grow. How can someone be productive or create something beautiful in life if they are not at peace with themselves and having peaceful and nourishing thoughts and relationships?

I have seen many people in very unstable relationships struggling in other areas of life because their emotions were not at peace, and there was no understanding. They were losing too much energy fighting with partners or family because of jealousy or other reasons, and they could not go much further this way. Sooner or later this kind of relationship breaks up because peace was not there.

It reminds me also the words of Thich Nhat Hanh, the Zen master:

"Many people think excitement is happiness... But when you are excited you are not peaceful. True happiness is based on peace."

There are many ways we can return to our original state of peace. For instance, whenever you notice you are irritated or feel a negative emotion arriving, go for a little mindful walk in nature and breathe fresh air. Walk as long as you need to feel calmness and balance again. Gardening and touching the earth is another excellent way of returning to your original state of peace. The Earth is always here to support us. If you cannot go for a mindful walk in nature or do not have a garden, you might like to start a yoga practice which can bring you immense relief. Start listening to nature tracks, meditation music and to the sound frequencies that will help you to restore your sense of peace. To this I have dedicated an entire chapter later in the book.

Finally, when we return to our original state of peace we are ready to experience an expanded love, beyond ourselves or someone else. We offer our love to all living beings and creatures.

Every Smile Counts

What is going to happen to us as a human species? As time passes and we evolve, the next generations will be forced to deal with the consequences of what is happening now both with humanity and with Mother Nature. Human destruction is happening every day, but divine intervention is already happening, and a massive soul migration has started on our planet. Of course, we are not doing this work alone. I know there are many angels working here with us, and the same power that guides the stars guides us too!

For us to change any given situation and shift the vibration of our planet, all we think and do as individuals matters. Each and every thought and action changes the vibration. Energy is exponential, it multiplies. Each and every smile counts. It does not matter if we don't know how we are going to make things happen, we just need to get ourselves ready. The Universe will respond to us in ways we could never have imagined. You don't need to try to understand it, but there is a supreme intelligence beyond us all. Just smile, shift your energy into love, and be ready. That is the way we manifest.

Some people might ask: How can I smile when I feel sad or when life has been so unfair to me? How can I make decisions out of love when I've never received love?

I will answer this question in details and I can tell you that many people have done it. From their toughest experiences, they made it through to the other side. They reached into this space of forgiveness and compassion and healed their pain, transmuting their suffering and the suffering of others into love. We don't need to be a victim of our past or carry it all our lives—we can turn it around and transform it. This is exactly the power of love.

In my own experience, every time I was faced with a challenge, I was not afraid, even though I didn't know how I was going to get through it. I was ready and present and had courage and faith. And the Universe always provided everything I needed. I was never left alone, I just had to trust the Universe. Each time, incredible situations and circumstances just happened, on all scales, both small and big events, with all the tiny details taken care of. I have no doubt that there is a divine intelligent force behind everything, and that this intelligence is made out of love.

These seeds are in you, in me, and in everyone. We can access love through our own nature, by activating this power in our hearts.

Secretly, I would often call, *"Gaia, Pacha mama, Mother Earth! Paramapurusha, Father Universe! This is so great, no words to describe your love and beauty! Thank you so much for everything... I love you so much!"*

I could say it to myself a thousand times and it would never be enough. I could spend my entire life saying thank you and I love you, but it would still not be enough. The more I open myself and my heart, the more I discover an infinite ocean of love. I know that I am both nothing and everything. The paradoxes of existence! I am the child of Mother Earth and of Father Universe. I am a lucky child to have such parents, to be born and to recognize my highest and deepest love for those who gave us life. Father, Mother, I love you. We are all brothers and sisters here on this planet.

The more I open myself and my heart, the more I discover an infinite ocean of love. I know I can always call my Mother and Father, and they will always be there for me. Mother Earth and Father Universe can never die. They gave us everything. They gave us our existence. We —and all living beings—owe our existence to the creative power of love. When we nurture and recognize this love inside ourselves, we can experience life from another dimension. I have been loving the Earth as my mother and the Universe as my father for a long time, along with my blood parents and ancestors. I honor them with deep love and gratitude, as much as I can, every day.

Have courage my children, brothers and sisters—courage is beautiful! Let us honor, recognize, and love our divine parents as we do our blood parents and ancestors. Let us forgive anything that needs to be forgiven. Forgive and let it go to the past where it belongs, so that we can experience love inside ourselves and pass to another level of understanding and expansion in this present moment. Let us have the courage to create new, loving experiences in our lives, right here and now.

Connect with this dimension of the present moment, call on your loving Mother Earth and Father Universe and see how they are here for you. Having an adult body does not necessarily mean we are mature in mind and spirit. We could technically be an adult but still act foolishly. If we could not see clearly before, it was because our mind was too foggy, too busy with minuscule dimensions of existence, such as small problems that were made big.

What humanity is lacking most is honesty, creativity, courage, compassion and trust in the Universe. How can we be completely humble and surrender to this divine energy? How can we surrender to this feeling, unafraid to show our vulnerability? Courage is essential in exposing our truth and our sensibility to others.

Now is time for us to go deeper into understanding our existence, to open our heart and see who we truly are. In fact, we must return to our inner child to accept and love ourselves. Just as Jesus said:

> *"Truly I tell you, unless you change and become like little children, you will never enter the kingdom of heaven."*
> *Matthew 18:3*

You do not need to be Christian or follow any religion to be able to recognize this. Just give love to the inner child inside of you. Transformation is happening constantly, and the child within you will never die. Understand that God, love and truth brings us all to the same point. They are just different words that arrive at the same place: —the center of our being and our heart space. You don't need to have a broad intellectual scope; very much the opposite, you just need to be free and authentic, to be in contact with nature, and follow the path of love and truth inside of you.

3. SEEDS OF GRATITUDE AND FORGIVENESS

"The attitude of gratitude is the highest yoga."
Yogi Bhajan

> *"It is through gratitude for the present moment that the spiritual dimension of life opens up."*
> *Eckhart Tolle*

Being in the present makes us aware of its greatness. For me, life is all about perception and gratitude. Even though there is so much we cannot perceive, there is still so much to be grateful for. Gratitude is one of my most beloved seeds—and my favorite door to enter Dharma.

Dharma means "cosmic law and order." It can be applied to all mental constructs or perceptions. It is also the term for all "phenomena." Dharma can also be understood as the "right way of living," or as a body of doctrine pertaining to the purification and moral transformation of human beings. In Buddhism philosophy it is said that there are more than 84,000 doors to enter the Dharma!

There is a little Buddhist story in which a man was hit by an arrow in the forest. He was deeply hurt and bleeding, but before anyone could help him he wanted to understand the circumstances of the event that had taken place, which was causing him so much pain. He wanted to know why such a thing had happened to him, where the arrow came from, what material it was made of, how it had happened and so on. Despite his restless search for knowledge, he died before he got all the answers.

The moral of this story is: do not try to understand things with your mind, not even your pain and suffering. We lose too much of our precious lifetime trying to understand. When we are hurt, we might waste too much time thinking and questioning why or how this could have happened to us. By doing so we are also feeding our painful memories and emotions. All we need is true forgiveness and to take care of ourselves and focus on our healing.

Life is short, and if we try to find all the answers, we will most likely die before we do so. Therefore, we do not need to understand everything, we just need more acceptance, humbleness, forgiveness, love, compassion and gratitude. A world without pain and suffering does not exist. Love and compassion are born from suffering. The light of life cannot be seen and appreciated without darkness. The polarities of life, such as positive and negative energies, are not a contradiction of each other, rather they complement each other. Nothing can exist separated.

The Universe offers us so many opportunities to experience all that is beautiful and sacred. We can be grateful for all our experiences, even those that cause us pain and suffering, and so we learn from them.

But how can we be grateful for negative experiences?

There is always something to be grateful for in every experience. In some very painful experiences, some of us may not be able to find gratitude. But if you look deep, you will see that all of life's painful and traumatic experiences are just memories stored inside the body. Those memories are not your true being. Memories can be forgiven, so you can turn the page and write a new story. You do not need to carry this sorrow inside of yourself for the rest of your life. There are many other things to be grateful for in life and it is always possible to water seeds of gratitude inside ourselves. In the beginning these seeds might be small, but as you keep watering them every day, they will grow strong and beautiful in your heart. Gratitude can be found in the present moment as an opportunity for the soul to be open for love.

Back in Brazil when I was 15 years old, I had a serious accident while riding a horse at a friend's farm. This accident turned out to be a blessing, and it would be one of the most important events of my young life. My right foot was badly injured, and I could not return to school in the United States, where I was living. I vividly remember holding my foot for six hours, all the way to the hospital, and wondering what would happen to me. By the time we arrived, it was so painful that I cried to the doctor, "Please, give me something so I can rest. I am so grateful that it was only my foot, not my whole leg, or my spine. But, please, I need to sleep now." That day, I reached the breaking point, I couldn't take it anymore.

I was both physically hurt and emotionally exhausted. I remember waking up from surgery in the intensive care unit of the biggest public hospital in town. It was a big ward with several beds; and machines were beeping continuously. I looked around and saw the other patients, they all seemed much more hurt than I was.

The next day I went home, and a few weeks later, due to complications, I needed a second operation and later, another one. After the third surgery, I was informed that my foot was developing gangrene because there was almost no blood circulating through it. The doctor said we could not wait much longer, and that in three days I would have my foot amputated, cut off from my body. Despite being just 15 years old, my attitude was not one of fear or despair, but of immense gratitude towards my foot, and for my whole body. I spent the long days at the hospital saying thank you and goodbye to my foot, giving it as much love as I could, massaging it all the time, even though I had lost all sensation and it was turning black. I was cleaning its wounds, full of compassion.

Three days later, the doctor came back and said they could wait a week longer as my foot was suddenly responding better. A week passed and I kept doing what I was doing, giving so much love to my foot. And when the time came again, there was no need to cut off my foot. Without knowing it, I was healing myself! This experience was such a blessing. This accident had such an impact on me and I couldn't have imagined how much I would grow from it. When I left the hospital, the doctor said it would take many months for me to walk again, and a minimum of six months of physiotherapy for the circulation in my ankles to go back to normal.

For many months, I was not able to put my leg down as my foot would immediately become swollen. And so I lay down on my bed with pillows underneath my leg, giving myself time to heal. When I was finally able to learn to walk again, I was so afraid to put my weight on my leg because it was very weak. I had lost all my muscle, my right leg was so thin, and my fragile ankle had lost all movement. I was supposed to do physiotherapy. Instead, following my feelings, I decided to do it my own way and did not go to even one session. I simply went for long walks in the forest, walking up and down the mountain near my home. There, I could breathe and be with the trees, and that was more healing and pleasurable for me. Up on the mountain I could also enjoy the great views, appreciating the sky, the ocean, and the fresh air. I did that twice a day, and after three months I was able to walk almost perfectly! The doctor was very surprised by my rapid progress.

And inside of me? An immense feeling of gratitude to be able to walk again!

Do we really need to suffer to be deeply grateful for the simple fact that we can walk? Do we have to be sick or hurt in order to become more conscious of everything that is available to us and everything we can be grateful for? Did I need to pass through pain to be able to be grateful?

This accident was definitely one of the most important events of my life and of my early years; a great opportunity of growth for my spirit. From that time, I started planting so many seeds of gratitude inside myself. I would never again take for granted the simple act of walking. I am so grateful for it that I would even say it was one of the best things that has ever happened to me.

It is when we overcome struggles that we are able to fully appreciate life. But I didn't need more pain and suffering in order to be grateful. I had learned the lesson. From then on, my vow was not to forget to be grateful for the rest of my days on Earth.

This accident was the first major struggle I experienced which turned out to be a blessing. It was no one but my own faith and gratitude encouraging myself to get back up. From then on, I understood that every experience can be an opportunity to learn and grow. Of course, we will always face challenges during the course of life, but everything can turn into an opportunity for consciousness to expand. We can open our eyes and be more grateful for everything in life. It seems that the more I cultivate seeds of gratitude in me, the more I remember to be always deeply grateful. I don't want to live in forgetfulness.

GRATITUDE & BEAUTY

"Every day, think as you wake up, today I am fortunate to be alive, I have a precious human life, I am not going to waste it. I am going to use all my energies to develop myself, to expand my heart out to others; to achieve enlightenment for the benefit of all beings. I am going to have kind thoughts towards others, I am not going to get angry or think badly about others. I am going to benefit others as much as I can."
14th Dalai Lama

For many years, I kept the Dalai Lama's words hanging on my wall so that I would not forget them when waking up. It was a reminder of the wonderful seed of gratitude.

I feel deeply grateful for all the people who are planting gratitude in their hearts. I am grateful for all the grateful people in this world! Learning to be grateful is one of the best things we can do for ourselves and for others. We can have gratitude for anyone, even people we haven't met, such as authors or musicians who have contributed to who we are and to the expansion of our consciousness. We sometimes forget to express this gratitude towards others, and especially towards Mother Earth and the Universe. But the more we do, the more this loving energy will shine on us.

Do you remember those who were grateful for you when you helped them out? What about those who helped you when you needed it?

Gratitude for the beauty of nature is an amazing seed to plant. When we develop the ability to recognize beauty, we start to realize that it is everywhere. It is all around and within us. Beauty is the reflection and manifestation of love. One assured way to observe beauty is by simply going into nature and seeing how Earth is so incredibly amazing and generous to us. As a result, we realize that love is everywhere!

Once, I was lying in the snow on top of a mountain in the Swiss Alps, and even though it was winter, it almost felt like a summer day. There was snow everywhere, but the sun was high up in the sky, shining strongly, so I took off my jacket and fully appreciated the beauty around me. I was there, totally in the present moment, and that single moment became magical. When we recognize beauty, we start to see the magic in every moment.

On that mountain, I was so grateful to Mother Nature for all that she provides. It is about realizing these simple things, the things that come naturally to us and that we often forget to appreciate and be grateful for. Most of us only tend to appreciate something once we do not have it anymore, or almost lose it. But you do not need to turn blind to appreciate the fact that you can see beauty with your eyes. We can express gratitude every day of our lives by awakening our consciousness to the beauty that is around us.

On top of that mountain, I said to myself:

"I am grateful for my eyes that allow me to see all the colors, the mountains, the flowers, and forests of the Earth. I am grateful for my ears that allow me to hear the blowing winds, the crashing waves, the birds singing and all the beautiful music and sounds that exist. I am grateful for my voice that allows me to express myself freely and to communicate and sing... I am grateful for this very air that I am breathing..."

I could go on and on, being grateful for each and every cell of my body, and for the entire Universe. Until the day I leave this planet, I will never stop saying thank you to everyone and everything. We can always find things to be grateful for. The biggest and most evident one is being alive and for all that we do have in life. Even for the pain and all the things we do not understand.

Gratitude is the key that opens all doors.

Gratitude is the beam that has guided me in my darkest hours. I am also grateful for the opportunity to learn from all kinds of suffering. It has made me appreciate life, family and friends, and every moment even more. Our suffering reminds us that time can heal everything; it is part of our growth, and from the moment one begins to feel gratitude, the suffering immediately starts healing.

It is essential to be grateful for all opportunities that life presents to us. Be grateful thousands of times, millions of times, infinite times. Keep caring for yourself and you will have so much energy and life around you. Cultivate those seeds inside yourself, shower yourself with gratitude every single day. Cleanse yourself with gratitude simply by saying "Thank You" to yourself, to everyone and to everything. Repeat it internally, using it as a mantra. By repeating "Thank You" it becomes a powerful cleansing program for your system, and you will be able to share the fruits of your garden with many others.

Go deeper into all that you can be grateful for, and all that you have, and all the opportunities in your life. You may like to take a piece of paper and start writing down everything you can be grateful for. Do it on a regular basis and you will find there is an infinite source of things you can be grateful for. You will feel as if there is a rainfall of blessings coming down on you, but you were not experiencing it before because of the umbrella of your ego that was covering you. Let it go! Take out the umbrella of the ego, connect to the present moment and let this blissful rain fall over you.

Not long ago, I sat in a circle with some special friends. It was a full moon and we were all so happy to connect and share such a moment together. We played laughing games and we then decided to do a circle of gratitude. Each person would say a few words about anything he or she was grateful for in life. We kept going around the circle for many rounds, in a meditative way. It turned out to be so amazing and beautiful! We were incredibly happy to share all the precious gems of the heart with each other. Such a heart-opening circle! We were practicing inner gardening together, planting and cultivating beautiful seeds of gratitude.

Connecting to Nature

When we are awakening, we truly begin to see the magnificence of nature. The blue sky, the colorful flowers, the melodious birds; we can open our eyes to this magical life. This is possible by reconnecting with Mother Earth, because everything starts and ends with her. We will all return to Mother Earth sooner or later, after we are gone from this physical body. Reconnecting with Mother Earth is a very important practice.

Every time I see the beauty of nature, it feels like I am in a sanctuary. To me, nature is like a temple. If we look deeply into the beauty, we will see there are so many temples around us, hidden within incredible natural landscapes. It does not matter where you are—even in the city, you can also appreciate this beauty by looking to the sky. If you practice looking deeply to our Earth, you may hear the voice of the river, the waterfall, the ocean, the mountains, the trees, the birds and so on. You can immerse yourself back into your true nature.

One day, on a beautiful morning walk near my home in Switzerland, I stopped by a thin stream to wash my face. The water was so fresh and pure, and I was reminded of the Zen master Thich Nhat Hanh. He tells a story of how one morning he woke up and when he opened his eyes he smiled. He knew he was alive and that he had 24 new hours to live! He stood on the earth, feeling the soles of his feet connecting with the ground. He felt how the earth was supporting him beneath his feet. He was feeling present in his body and aware of his breath. He then walked slowly to the bathroom to wash his face, appreciating every step as if he was kissing the earth through the soles of his feet. An extraordinary experience! He opened the tap and touched the water. The water in his hands gave him such a feeling of immense gratitude, and he appreciated where the water was coming from. He was feeling its sacredness, imagining and appreciating how the beautiful source of water reached his bathroom. From the very moment he woke up that morning, he was already experiencing the miracle of life!

After hearing this, I was much more able to honor the water, washing my face in mindfulness as well as honoring the earth I walked on. Can we remind ourselves to wake up in such a way? If we all could wash our face and walk in the morning the way the Zen master does, if we could have gratitude for all the simple, amazing things, what a life we could experience and create! This is just an observation of how a simple act can change depending on how we feel and think about it, and how grateful we are. Externally, an action done by two different people can look the same, but the internal experience can be totally different. It all depends on how conscious we are of each and every moment. We can bring this awareness into our actions and train our minds to return to the present moment, cultivating seeds of gratitude.

If we really want to appreciate life, we have to look deeply at everything we are doing. One day, skiing down a mountain in the Alps, I suddenly stopped when I found a small hut immersed in the snow. There was no one there and so I sat down on a bench in front of the hut, taking in the magical mountain scenery. While sitting there, I felt how much I missed living in tiny little huts, like I had in Nepal and the Philippines. I remembered how happy I was living in small spaces and having nothing, just being with Mother Earth.

Since moving to Switzerland, the situation had changed, given we had such a big house to renovate and take care of. We had to buy many things for our new home. We renovated the place — I called it the New Energy School — and turned an abandoned 350-year-old chalet into a comfortable home. Of course I was grateful for it, but I truly missed living free in nature. I never wanted to be trapped in accumulating material things. I missed having less and feeling free.

Whenever I could escape from the hard work of the renovation, I never missed the chance to admire the impressive mountains of the Alps. Majestic and breath-taking, the white mountains created such a beautiful contrast with the vibrant blue sky overhead. I could feel my heart beating strongly with every breath while I looked deeply at that scenery.

Looking at the magnificent mountains, I could truly enjoy the silence of the present moment and feel so happy, being totally grateful for it. And so, in humbleness, truly absorbed their beauty and force, and felt the warmth of the sun. *Please, mountains help me to be like you, solid and strong! To have strength to pass through all the challenges and bad weather!*

Getting in tune with myself in these precious moments, I was able to enjoy solitude. It's important to take time for ourselves, to pause and reflect, and feel. At that moment, I was able to truly be with the mountains, to feel them in such a deep way that I became one with them. In silence, I appreciated each minute and allowed it to be eternal and to bring me peace. Each opportunity we have, we can be grateful for.

Transformation

Nothing ever really begins or ends, it just transforms. Transformation is happening all the time. Your body will be transformed into dust again and again, as in every living being's life cycle. Because you are alive, you have the power to transform your thoughts, feelings, and emotions. I know there are many people awakening on our planet, and there is already a lot of transformation happening. There are so many opportunities for us to grow and understand our experiences in life.

When you feel mentally ready to transcend your pain, a transformation from pain to power can begin. From that moment on:

Your past is no longer a place of pain but a source of power.

I have met people who have done just this, and they were able to have a great impact on others. They were able to overcome their suffering by choosing to forgive and see the light and beauty of life again. These stories are very inspiring and beautiful. On the opposite side, we also hear stories of people whose love for someone turned into pain and hate, leading to more suffering.

Why do we hold on to pain? Why don't we feel happy? Why do we push ourselves to be so busy?

If we lead a very busy life and do not take time to slow down, transformation will not happen. Silence and rest are fundamental for the growth and healing process. Are we ready for transformation? Are we willing to expand our potential? To plant in our inner garden and discover the essence of true beauty within ourselves? Will we manifest it as true reality?

A caterpillar must confront these same questions. For the caterpillar to become a butterfly, it must undergo a deep psychological and physiological transformation. As a caterpillar, it lives a very basic, primordial life. If the caterpillar is lucky enough to harness energy and strength, it develops the ability to create a relatively safe and peaceful place for itself to become something much greater. Within the cocoon, the caterpillar has time to go inwards and grow, to reassess its position in the environment. Upon awakening from this state of slumber and meditation within the cocoon, it emerges as something reborn. It manifests back into the world as a beautiful symbol of transformation and expanded potential.

The life cycle of the caterpillar represents something much more immense and powerful. It is a living example of bringing the essence of beauty into existence through personal transformation. We can all tap into the butterfly within us, incubate ourselves in a cocoon, and allow ourselves to go through our own transformation and awakening. In our human state, we have the power to undergo this rebirth. We can constantly evolve, as the magical beauty of our nature is impermanence. This impermanence is not only within us, but is omnipotent in the rest of the Universe too.

We cannot stop evolution. Though it might take millions of years for nature to restore itself, it is just a matter of time—for there is a supreme intelligence beyond all life and existence, beyond our human limitations and understanding, and this intelligence governs our lives. The human body, the stars in the universe, and everything on Earth are all in a constant cycle of change. The only thing we can be sure of is that life is pure transformation. Everything is always evolving and transforming in a continuous and never-ending process, and consciousness will shift. Nothing is permanent, and understanding this will also bring us a sense of non-attachment to our pain and suffering. It's when we realize we want to stop being a caterpillar but instead become a butterfly that this process of transformation can begin.

The Art of Non-Doing

Sometimes, it is important to stop everything completely and wrap yourself up in stillness like the caterpillar. Just relax, lie down in the sun, and bask in the warmth of the rays. *Simply do nothing and just be, allowing healing to take place.* Sometimes we are so wrapped up in work and we need time to slow down, to go back into ourselves and rest as the caterpillar does, to allow transformation to happen. Although being and feeling productive is important, it is also important to just stop and do nothing. Rest your body and mind, and create cycles of doing and of non-doing.

This time of non-doing is very precious. It's a time to be light and free: no overthinking, no overdoing, just being. When we clear the mind of thoughts and worries, inspiration and creativity appear, just as clouds disappear and the sun shines strongly.

The moment of presence is the moment we get inspired.

Constant and excessive thinking does not benefit the mind or body. It is all about focusing on the quality of your thoughts rather than the quantity. We might have many thoughts and ideas, but what is really important is what we choose to focus on. Even if it is only one simple idea, our productivity can improve greatly when we are consciously aware of it. This is more valuable than hundreds of ideas getting lost in the air and in the mind.

Still, there is certainly no such thing as *non-doing*. Even when you are sleeping you are doing something. If you're taking a sunbath, you're absorbing the sunlight. If you're looking into a beautiful landscape, or at the sky and the clouds, you're still doing something; you are appreciating life. As Shakespeare once wrote: "There are more things in heaven and earth, Horatio, than are dreamt of in your philosophy."

Just like a rainbow that appears for a brief period, let us be reminded of how beautiful and ephemeral this magical world is. Pause and reflect upon this question: When was the last time you truly looked up into the sky and stopped to appreciate its greatness?

FORGIVENESS

One of the best things we can do for ourselves is to let go and forgive the past, and all old hurts. By forgiving ourselves, our parents, families, ancestors, and others, we can heal our past and create a better life on this planet. Then we can be free, playful, and enthusiastic again, to share our creativity and wisdom with the world.

We need to forgive and let go of the past in order to fully live in the present moment. It's only when we forgive that we can set ourselves free.

Painful past stories are only memories replaying in the mind, which do not allow us to be happy and free. It is a prison, and our pain and anger become our own cell. This happens when we identify with the sufferings of the past. We forgive first of all because we want to be free. We want to free ourselves.

We can leave the past behind. If I can free myself, you too can free yourself and experience something new, to create something better for your future, our future, and the future of humanity. At some point we get tired of all those stories of pain and suffering and want to make something better from our lives. Now is the right time, the right place, and the right book. There are no coincidences. There is an infinite intelligence that guides the stars and guides us too.

Let us go on a journey of dreams! Let us do it not only for ourselves but also for our past, present and future generations. We can let go of all those painful stories that we have carried for so long, consciously or not, from our past and from our ancestors. We do not need to be carrying this pain and suffering anymore. We can get rid of it because we want to be happy and free. This is our birth right!

Many of us spend years holding on to painful memories. Can you recognize how much time you have spent holding on to your pain? We can be attached to the memories of the past or we can choose to forgive those painful memories, to cultivate gratitude and compassion and move on. We can forgive ourselves and others, in humbleness, for our mistakes and ignorance. We can be grateful for life, for Mother Earth, and everything that has been provided for us. The transformation from pain to power is attainable! To get there, compassion, understanding and forgiveness must occur.

Forgiveness is necessary in order for you to liberate the memories that are blocking your energy and inhibiting you from fully experiencing the present moment. Only you can free yourself. Nobody else can do it for you. Only you have the ability to forgive from your heart and turn the page, to let go of the old and be ready for the new.

When we surrender and trust, we know that life is always transforming and evolving. We can transform everything—this is the power of love. And when we cultivate and nurture gratitude for the simple things around us, more gratitude will come, spreading seeds into our garden of life. We can go deeper into understanding that forgiveness is mainly for ourselves. We forgive the past, and then we are free for something new.

Let go of the past and leave the pain where it belongs—in the past. You do not need seeds of pain and sorrow spoiling your abundant garden. We shall not identify as victims of life. We can stand up for ourselves when we feel we have had enough of pain and sorrow. The past is not something that constantly needs to be relived or analyzed. It just needs to be forgiven. It is an opportunity to learn and grow from experience.

If you want to be freed from your past, forgive yourself now! Not tomorrow, not in the future. In truth, past and future do not exist. The past is just memories replaying. The future is a mental projection. We can only live in the now. Start setting yourself free now! It is doable. You are not weak. You are not a victim of anything or anyone. You are a divine being. You can release the past and let go of all that no longer serves you. There is not much time to forgive before we die. You can forgive yourself and everyone else, and finally set yourself free! When you are finally free from your past memories and you forgive, you can truly be in the present moment. Forgiveness is a gift that you give to yourself.

You can overcome your sorrows and be grateful for life and all that you have been granted at this moment. Remember: we can choose and cultivate all the seeds in our inner garden. Plant seeds of gratitude and forgiveness, water them carefully every day and see the beauty in your life flourish. You have infinite potential, you just need to believe in yourself. Step out and fly! Take flight knowing that you are no longer caged in the prison of your own mind.

4.
SEEDS OF COMPASSION

"Don't underestimate yourself. You have the ability to wake up. You have the ability to be compassionate. You just need a little bit of practice to be able to touch the best that is in you. Enlightenment, mindfulness, understanding, and compassion are in you. Very simple practices – such as meditative walking, mindful breathing, or washing your dishes mindfully –
make it possible for you to leave hell and touch the positive seeds that are within you."
Thich Nhat Hanh

The Happiest Man in the World

Once, I read an article about 'The Happiest Man in the World,' Matthieu Ricard, a Buddhist monk. He participated in a 12-year brain study on meditation and compassion led by Richard Davidson, a neuroscientist from the University of Wisconsin, USA. His head was hooked to 256 sensors and found that when he was meditating on compassion his mind was unusually light. The scans showed that his brain was producing a level of gamma waves—those linked to consciousness, attention, learning and memory—never before reported in neuroscience literature. The scans also showed excessive activity in his brain's left prefrontal cortex compared to its right counterpart, allowing him an abnormally large capacity for happiness and a reduced propensity towards negativity. To Matthieu Ricard, it was clear:

> *"Simply be a compassionate person and your brain will produce high amounts of happiness hormones."*

Compassion and altruism were the answer. His practices were very simple: meditate every day on compassion. Many of us nowadays take pills or drugs to artificially create a sensation of happiness. Indeed, what we are really missing is compassion in our lives.

From Davidson's study, I arrived at the conclusion that all our suffering, sadness and depression come mainly from a deep lack of compassion. Thinking about yourself all the time is exhausting and stressful, and ultimately leads to unhappiness. This is the ultimate spiritual ignorance of our civilization. Why have humans been suffering for so long? Because we do not cultivate enough compassion.

If we want to be happy, we should strive for "benevolence," which will not only make us feel better, but will make others feel better as well. That is not to say you should let people take advantage of you, but you should strive to be kind to all. If your mind is filled with benevolence, compassion and solidarity, this will lead you to happiness. No doubt.

While science has made progress in treating pathologies of the human mind, far less research exists to date on positive qualities of the human mind including compassion, altruism and empathy. Yet they are innate to us and lie at the very core of our common humanity. Our capacity to feel compassion has ensured the survival and thriving of our species over millennia. The Center for Compassion and Altruism Research and Education (CCARE) at Stanford University School of Medicine in the US, was created with this objective and works with a number of prominent neuroscientists, behavioral scientists, geneticists and biomedical researchers to closely examine the physiological and psychological correlation between compassion and altruism. All these are subjects of meditation. The Dalai Lama has also been one of the biggest sponsors of this research.

Unfortunately, because depression affects millions of people worldwide, it is not in the interest of the big pharmaceutical companies that people find ways to heal themselves without chemicals, free of cost. The epidemiology of depression has been largely studied. In fact, depression is a major cause of morbidity worldwide.

Take, for example, the historical moment of Covid-19, with a media that emphasizes the death of a great number of people by the virus. In real numbers, it kills only a very small percentage of those who are contaminated. Great social disorder happened worldwide and governments implemented fears on the population, with so much political and scientific confusion. Indeed, there has never been a widespread knowledge of how many more people are dying of hunger every day, or in the wars and violence that keep going on in many parts of the world, or of cancer and depression and so on. All of this mirrors our collective consciousness. For those who are awakening, let's meditate on compassion. More than ever, the world needs love and healing.

Meditating on Compassion

Meditation helps us to cultivate compassion in our inner garden. Matthieu Ricard says that it does not require years of studying and practicing. In merely a few weeks, anyone can experience increased daily positive emotions, reduced depressive symptoms, and increased life satisfaction by practicing meditation. Compassion is not dependent on any formal meditation; it is all in our hearts. One can simply decide to be more compassionate, and get involved in doing benevolent and altruistic work.

Davidson's study found that just 20 minutes of daily meditation can make people happier. Try it and you will experience increasing positive effects in your life. It may be sitting meditation, walking or active meditation. With time, mindfulness and compassion can be extended to your daily activities. If we keep cultivating compassion, we too can become a "happiness pro."

Everyone can have a lighter mind due to the potential for goodness in every human being. Meditation is a pleasant way to change how the brain works. It can boost people's happiness in the same way exercise can build muscle. We can start by focusing on our breathing and being conscious of the present moment, rather than dwelling on the past or future. The key is to focus on the breath and just let any intrusive thoughts pass through your mind like clouds in the sky. Observe and recognize how they come and go, and just let everything go. Observe the impermanence of all Dharmas. Your breath is your power source—feel it profoundly.

If you want to go deeper, as you breathe in, feel you are breathing love into yourself, and to all the cells of your body. And as you breathe out, feel you are breathing gratitude towards all life.

If you can take a few conscious breaths in such a way, for a few minutes every day, you are watering seeds of kindness, compassion and love in yourself. Just like any skill, when we practice it enough it becomes more of a lifestyle. As we continue these practices and grow older, we gain more wisdom. This is especially true if we learn to be more generous, altruistic, and peaceful every day.

Are you ready to go deeper into your heart? To raise up your energy to your ultimate potential? To cultivate and grow these seeds in your beautiful garden?

Understanding Compassion

Not long ago, I was speaking with someone who, to my surprise, did not know the meaning of the word "compassion." I realized it was not only him, but that there are millions of people around the world who do not know what compassion truly means. In recent years, compassion has received more scientific interest, and it is mainly defined by five elements:

1. recognizing suffering in others;
2. understanding the common humanity of this suffering;

3. feeling emotionally connected with the person who is suffering;
4. tolerating difficult feelings that may arise;
5. being motivated to help the person who is suffering.

According to the Oxford English Dictionary, the word "compassion" stems from the Latin "*compati*", meaning "to suffer with." In literature, compassion involves feelings for persons who are suffering and being motivated to help them.

Compassion is fundamental in Buddhist philosophy and it is defined as "an openness to the suffering of others with a commitment to relieve it." It is, in fact, emphasized by all the main world religions. Compassion is not only seen as an emotional reaction, but also as a response to reason and wisdom.

Compassion is not only for those who are close to us, but also for those we do not know. One can feel compassion for those one might never meet. Compassion can be extended to all living beings and creatures. Self-compassion also includes *kindness* (being kind and non-judgmental towards the self rather than self-critical), *mindfulness* (which involves observing painful feelings in mindful awareness rather than over-identifying with them), and *common humanity* (seeing one's suffering as part of the human condition rather than an isolated case).

The 14th Dalai Lama said:

"Genuine compassion must have both wisdom and loving-kindness. That is to say, one must understand the nature of the suffering from which we wish to free others (this is wisdom), and one must experience deep intimacy and empathy with other sentient beings (this is loving-kindness)."

Compassion is different from empathy. Empathy allows us to take the perspective of another person and feel the same emotions. Compassion is when those feelings and thoughts include the desire to help. It is felt specifically in response to suffering, whereas empathy may apply to a wider range of situations. For example, one could feel empathy with someone else's anger, fear or joy. It is the vicarious experience of another's emotions. Compassion is an emotion in its own right. It is broader than empathy because it can be felt for humanity at large rather than only in relation to specific interpersonal encounters.

Pity, on the other hand—despite having similarities to compassion—does not include an inclination to help. On the contrary, pity implies that one sees someone as unworthy of help, or at least involves showing condescension towards them. Altruism has a greater focus on behavioral acts, and it is a result of compassion. Nonetheless, compassion and altruism are the fruits of love.

Compassion's Benefits

> *"When we focus on others, our world expands. Our own problems drift to the periphery of the mind and so seem smaller, and we increase our capacity for connection — or compassionate action."*
> *Daniel Goleman*

Anyone who is interested in positive psychology—the psychology of happiness and human flourishing—knows that connecting with others in a meaningful way improves mental and physical health, often speeding up recovery from disease.

Energetically speaking, the Universe reflects everything we are internally. For compassionate people, the Universe is very loving, kind, and generous in return. The energy we put out into the world is what we will receive. Scientifically speaking, compassion may have aided our survival because of its tremendous benefits for both our physical and mental health and overall well-being.

Compassion can improve our life in several ways, such as reducing the risk of heart disease, reducing stress and strengthening the immune response in the body.

The reason a compassionate lifestyle leads to greater psychological well-being may be explained by the fact that the act of giving appears to be as pleasurable, if not more so, than the act of receiving. A brain-imaging study headed by neuroscientist Jordan Grafman showed that the "pleasure centers" in the brain, the parts of the brain that are active when we experience pleasure, are equally active when we observe someone giving money to charity as when we receive money ourselves. Giving to others increases well-being above and beyond what we experience when we spend money on ourselves.

In a revealing experiment by Elizabeth Dunn at the University of British Columbia, participants received a sum of money and half of them were instructed to spend the money on themselves, while the other half was told to give to others. At the end of the study, participants who had gifted others felt significantly happier than those who had spent money on themselves.

Compassion leads to many health benefits, and a fascinating study by Cole and Fredrickson evaluated the levels of cellular inflammation in people who describe themselves as "very happy." Inflammation is at the root of cancer and other diseases and is generally high in people who live under a lot of stress. We might expect that inflammation would be lower for people with higher levels of happiness. However, this was only the case for certain "very happy" people. They found that people who were happy because they lived a "good life" (also known as "hedonic happiness") had high inflammation levels, but people who were happy because they lived a life of purpose or meaning (also known as "eudaimonic happiness") had low inflammation levels.

Another reason why compassion boosts our well-being is that it can help broaden our perspective beyond ourselves. Depression and anxiety are linked to a state of self-focus, a constant preoccupation with "me, myself, and I." When you do something for someone else, however, that state of self-focus shifts to a state of other-focus. Compassion improves our well-being by increasing our sense of connection to others. Social connection strengthens our immune system, helps us recover from disease faster, and prolongs our lifespan. People who feel more connected to others have lower rates of anxiety and depression, have higher self-esteem, are more empathetic, trusting and cooperative, and as a consequence, others are more open to trusting and cooperating with them.

Therefore, social connectedness generates a virtuous circle of emotional and physical well-being. Unfortunately, the opposite is also true for those who lack social connectedness. Low social connection has been generally associated with declines in physical and psychological health, as well as a higher propensity for antisocial behavior that leads to further isolation.

How happy we are in our relationships has a powerful influence on our health. Taking care of your body is important but tending to your relationships is a form of self-care too. A life of meaning and purpose is one that is focused less on satisfying oneself and more on others. In short, it is a life rich in compassion.

Cultivating Compassion

Have you ever been moved to tears by another person's loving and compassionate behavior? Why are the lives of Buddha, Jesus, Mother Teresa, Martin Luther King Jr., and many masters so inspiring?

Once, in Brazil, my mother and I went for a walk on the beach around 7 a.m. It was a beautiful Sunday morning and the sun had woken up radiant. We were on our way when, to our surprise, we met a man sitting by the bus stop wearing a clown costume. He was so colorful, and wore a lot of makeup and had a beautiful smile on his face. In extreme curiosity, we approached and asked where he was going. He answered that he was on his way to the hospital to visit the sick patients who were in need of a smile. He said he wanted to make many people smile that day.

Many years have passed since our brief encounter with that compassionate stranger, but I've never forgotten him. I can still see his eyes shining and feel the happiness he brought to my heart. It is amazing to know that these kinds of people exist in the world. Maybe he had nothing else to give, such as money, but in my opinion, he was giving the most valuable things we truly have: time, attention, energy, hope, love and smiles to people who were in pain. It is so beautiful to witness human compassion and the altruism that comes with it.

Seeing someone helping another person creates a state of elevation in us. Helping is contagious:

acts of generosity and kindness create a chain reaction of goodness. Our acts of compassion uplift others and make them happy. I believe it is crucial for the evolution of humankind that all people, communities and governments have more access to compassion. It is time to start cultivating more of those seeds. The practice of compassion is just as important to health as physical exercise and a healthy diet.

I hope that soon the subject of compassion will be taught and applied more in schools, hospitals, prisons, and other community settings. These are some of the most precious and valuable seeds to cultivate in our garden of life. Cultivating compassion is also about learning to forgive. When we experience compassion, we truly leave the feeling of separation behind.

Tuning the Mind

We are free to make choices, although some people might not agree, and say something like, "I have no choice." If we think that way, it is an affirmation and we are already limiting ourselves. Perhaps we have been going down this path for such a long time that we have forgotten about our freedom. That is how we become a slave to our own mind.

When the mind is used in conjunction with the heart, it becomes a very powerful tool. Just as if we were playing an instrument, we can learn how to tune the mind and use it for our happiness. We either master the mind and it works for us, or the mind can become destructive and dangerous to both ourselves and others.

Why can human beings be so self-destructive? Why do so many people suffer from depression and mental disorders? We must first observe how the mind functions and operates, in order to understand.

The mind functions in conjunction with other parts of the body, such as our endocrine system. The mind also correlates with feelings, perception and interpretation. Compassion produces high amounts of serotonin and endorphins in the brain; it makes us happy, allowing us to guide our minds, thoughts and feelings to their happiest place.

Through compassion, we can make decisions based on what we truly love. We do not focus on our problems and fears anymore. We look for the beauty that is out there, waiting to be seen. It is not in thinking about the problems that we will find the solution. Quite the opposite; only when we let go of our thoughts will we find the solution and our problems will disappear.

We have heard this message of love for thousands of years from many generations, and in many ways. This message has come in different forms, teaching us lessons of forgiveness and compassion. In Western culture, we have learned that Jesus was crucified to ensure sins were forgiven and to purify the suffering of humanity.

An example of making a decision based in compassion is a shift away from our primitive survival mode. Nowadays in most parts of the world, we do not need to hunt or kill to survive. We can nurture compassion for the animals and for our own digestive system. We have so many resources and options to feed ourselves with delicious plant-based diets. More and more people are becoming conscious of this. Taking action by not eating meat or consuming dairy can make a big difference in our lives and to our planet.

When I met dear Deva Hanuman, my life partner, he had never experienced a vegetarian diet. He had grown up in a very carnivorous family. And he did not know he had so many other delicious options to feed himself in, a healthy and compassionate way. A similar thing also happened in my own family, and most of the families I knew. But I had to seek my own way of understanding and finding alternative ways of living on Earth. The moment I tried a vegetarian diet I understood that it is not only about love and compassion for the animals, but also for my own body, which would previously expend so much energy on digestion. In short, our bodies take at least one to three days to digest meat, during which time it is putrefying inside the body, while fruits take only half an hour if not mixed with other kinds of food; and vegetables around two to three hours. So it was about loving my body too, and helping the cells and my organs to work better, not overcharging them with toxins. My mind was much clearer and I had so much more energy. Going deeper I came to understand that this love was going further, to all the trees and animals that live in the forests, because the meat industry is one of the main causes of deforestation on our planet. I understood that the implication of eating meat goes far beyond what I initially imagined. If we, as a collective, keep eating meat, it can no longer be out of our ignorance in our collective level of consciousness. The moment we see so many of our acts and choices in the past were made out of ignorance, we must forgive ourselves and our ancestors too.

One might ask, what do hamburgers and chainsaws have in common? Both cause massive deforestation of tropical rainforests across the world. The beef industry is the biggest cause of deforestation in every country in the Amazonian region; experts have estimated that around 80% of deforestation in the Amazon is due to cattle ranching. And very few people are aware of it.

However, these numbers only account for the areas cleared for the creation of pastures and don't include land used to grow food being produced for cattle consumption. The Yale School of Forestry and Environmental Studies estimates that Brazil alone has 24 to 25 million hectares devoted to the production of soy, and 80% of this soy ends up as animal feed. It then stands that one of the quickest ways to prevent further deforestation in the Amazon is to decrease demand for Brazilian beef. However, that seems to be a far-off notion as worldwide demand for beef has only been increasing. Between 2010 and 2017, beef exports from the Amazon region rose 25% and continue to grow.

So how can we as individuals help protect the Amazon? The answer is simple: by changing our own eating habits. We must become conscious of the environmental impact of all our eating habits. If we replace meat with fruits, grains, or vegetables, the deforestation of the Amazon will decrease substantially. Brazil and other beef exporting countries would move away from the beef industry as demand and profits fall.

Cutting down on beef consumption alone won't end rainforest deforestation, but more than three fourths of the Amazon rainforests are being cut down almost exclusively because of it. Now, it seems like our responsibility to change our habits.

> *"By eating meat we share the responsibility of climate change, the destruction of our forests, and the poisoning of our air and water. The simple act of becoming a vegetarian will make a difference in the health of our planet."*
> *- Thich Nhat Hanh, The World We Have: A Buddhist Approach to Peace and Ecology*

We have access to much more information and knowledge than our ancestors did. Even if humanity hasn't yet accepted this wisdom, we do have the knowledge and we are only one step away from transformation. If we believe we're far from it then we will be far from it. If we believe we're close to it then we will be close to it. Our beliefs create our reality. You may even realize you are already in it. In fact, you *are* it.

5.

SEEDS OF AWARENESS

Let's focus on the seeds that we want to plant in our lives, and leave the past where it belongs. As we continue on this path of love, gratitude, joy and forgiveness, we will regenerate, recharge, and reset our system. We start over, clean everything, and pass the "anti-virus" of gratitude and forgiveness through our system. It heals and dissolves everything that does not serve us anymore.

We can do ourselves a favor: for our highest good and for the good of the entire planet, we can love ourselves. Any kind of problem we might face, or any difficulties we might endure, are related to our mental lenses and programs. It is not about our true being, because in our original and natural state, we are pure love. Free and playful, like little children.

Unfortunately, many people grow old and find that they did not take the time to consciously create a beautiful, meaningful life. They did not cultivate the garden of life from within, they did not plant seeds of love and compassion and did not spread these good seeds. Deep inside they may feel very frustrated and unhappy, whether they are conscious of it or not. Frustration gives rise to a lot of negative emotions, such as guilt, blame, and regret. Frustrated people often speak poorly about everything and everyone, and spend so much time and energy having negative thoughts. It is all because, in truth, they are not valuing themselves. It is not because of their insecurity and their inability to get what they wanted in due time. The hole is deeper than that. Frustration comes from a lack of self-love.

Maybe they lived their life for others, or they did not unlock their potential or nourish their own dreams. They are so frustrated, so full of ego that their heart space is closed up and they are trapped in their own minds. Criticism, aggression, and victimism are defense mechanisms of the ego, used to divert negative attention onto others. But if we recognize this, we can water the seeds of compassion in ourselves, and understand the nature of our pain. It is never too late, everything is possible! At any age and at any time we can awake. The Universe embraces everyone and is always waiting for our awakening.

The best way to help others is by first helping ourselves. We can heal our families and our planet by healing ourselves. We can love others by loving ourselves. When we love ourselves and reflect on who we are, we can harvest what we have been planting in our garden of life.

The best gift you can give to life, to others, to your ancestors, and to yourself is to be happy, to smile every day, and to be generous and compassionate.

The traditional thinking mode in this world limits our understanding and scope of action. Many people are not aware of this and have negative thoughts almost all the time, whispering negativity inside themselves, and with friends and family. Every time they think or say negative things they are watering these types of seeds in themselves. If we realized how negative it is to use our mind and speech in such a way, we would be more conscious of our thinking habits. Our mouth is a powerful, strong, influential instrument. Because of its power and ability to change the world, we need to be careful with it and use it for good. Continuous negative thinking creates sickness in your body and attracts problems in your life. It is a very destructive program that bugs our system.

We need to learn how to benefit from our thinking and speaking, and, by doing so, benefit others as well. We need to piece together sweet, compassionate, understanding thoughts and words and use them to grace others with beauty instead of using negative thoughts and words to judge others. What is the quality of your thoughts today and every day? These thoughts are powerful seeds that we cultivate inside ourselves. Our mind is fertile soil and will nourish any kind of thought we plant in it. Everything we think of will eventually grow and bear fruits, whether they are sweet and delicious or poisonous and deadly.

Look inside and ask yourself: Am I planting good seeds in the fertile soil of my mind? What kind of gardener am I? What have I been talking and thinking about recently? Am I thinking thoughts of love, compassion, and prosperity? Or am I planting seeds of poison with my beliefs and judgments? What is the quality of my thoughts, speech and actions? What do I want to feel when I grow older?

Finding the Way

So many people express that they do not know what to do with their life or which path to take. Recently, someone expressed exactly this concern to me, and I realized that this person was one of millions feeling the same way. They feel helpless, empty, and disconnected from nature. Have you ever felt this way? So many of us have, and it's important to observe this feeling and bring it into the light so that we can heal ourselves.

For me, one of the best ways to end this cycle of emotions and break any toxic pattern is to go on a big adventure or back into nature. This is especially important for those who work with technology, or who spend a lot of time in offices, with computers and cell phones. Technology definitely has its positive aspects, but it can pull us out of our center and roots. It is very important to use it carefully, because we might be over-connecting online and disconnecting from real life. It's important to break these patterns and spend a few hours every day—or full days, even weeks for those who can—in nature. It is essential to reconnect with it, since it is where we all come from. It reminds us of our origins and our true and only home. Detoxing from technology can be a very enriching experience, especially in nature, because it helps us reconnect with life.

One of our most toxic thought patterns is that we think we need a lot of money to be free, to be happy, or to enjoy life, which isn't true. What we really need is to be honest, to be true, to be authentic and courageous, to trust the Universe and to connect with our true nature. If we allow our hearts to guide us, everything we need will be provided to us. It is your heart that will guide you towards your true self and your true being. The love that guides your heart is not a romantic feeling related to a certain person. It's a universal love: loving life as we love ourselves and respecting life as we respect ourselves. The heart will always take you in the right direction, however, it needs a certain amount of courage to let go of old toxic patterns and habits.

How can we get ready to leave our comfort zone, open our wings, and fly? Many people are so afraid to fly with the wings of their dreams and imagination. Why? Because we try to hang on to security: to make more money, have more properties, to have a life with many pleasures and desires. We get trapped in the idea that we must adapt to the system, and if we don't we're a failure. But there are many other ways of being creative and happy in life. We don't have to follow the crowd or the mental programming we've been exposed to. We can create our own way, our own program, knowing that everyone is so unique, because it is diversity that makes life so beautiful.

Energy

Everything in the Universe is made up of energy. Quantum physics shows us how particles can seemingly disappear and reappear somewhere else in an instant. In our modern time, we have some knowledge of how energy works in the material and invisible worlds. Energy is not always visible to the naked eye, but it does exist, and no doubt it is very powerful.

Our bodies have a certain amount of energy according to our lifestyles and mental states. We are exchanging energy all the time, and with everyone around us. We can even sense and touch this mass of energy around a person. The energy fields around us contain a lot of electricity, and we can use this electricity like a phone uses a charger. When the battery on our phone is low, we immediately recharge it. Why do we charge our technological devices, but not ourselves?

The way we recharge ourselves is by going straight to the source of the power: Mother Nature.

How we interact with nature, how we feed our bodies, and the quality of our thoughts and our relationships all contribute to our energy levels. There are currents of energy and electricity that move in and around us. In our multidimensional body, we have many energy centers through which electricity circulates. In ancient Chinese medicine, these are called meridians; in Indian medicine they are called chakras. When energy flows freely without any blockages through the chakras, we experience a natural state of peace, health and happiness. If our energy centers get blocked, we can become sick.

All the physical and mental sickness in our world shows that most of us, as individuals and as societies, do not know how to channel these energies and life forces within ourselves. We are not connected to the source of power, and our energy becomes weak.

This life energy comes from all the elements that exist in the Universe. The four elements—water, fire, earth, air—are the very source of all of our scientific and technological developments. But how do we use these elements within our bodies? How can we connect to these energy sources and use them to increase our own energy levels?

If we learn the very basics about energy and its various fields, we would understand that energy is being exchanged all the time. Try to visualize your own energy field, the light around you, bright and shining, showering over your body. When you feel it from your heart, you are already receiving energy from the source. With this simple visualization, you can start to change the polarity in your body and mind, but repetition is the secret: keep visualizing in order to train your mind.

Your energy can also increase and shine brightly when you surround yourself with people who have positive energy. It feels really good to be around such people who recognize the source and energize themselves. The energy exchange then multiplies, and you feel better than ever.

Be aware, therefore, of what you are doing and where you are getting your energy from. When you feel your negative polarity and want to shift it, practice visualizing your energy field. I will share in later chapter, some visualization techniques that will allow you to bring this energy into balance and restore it.

The process requires learning to live in the present moment, which, ironically, means learning from the past but, at the same time, making the decision to leave the past behind. Going to the source of energy is much more pleasant than stealing it from others, and we can share our energy generously because the source is endless. With the right practices we can show people better ways of managing their energy systems. Remember, you can always go to the source to give and share this infinite energy.

The Power of Words

Are you conscious of how you communicate with others?

Sometimes we talk, but we don't realize the quality and the power of our words. If we speak without love and compassion, it can be very dangerous to both ourselves and others. Speaking in this way isolates and separates us. In fact, someone who is continuously tormented by the past and worried about the future, unhappy with their lives, can become mentally or physically sick.

Sickness sometimes can be the gift that shows us the need for transformation. It shows us that the way we had been living, thinking, speaking and acting was not the way of love.

In the path of love, our immune system performs at an optimum level, and the cells of our body vibrate joyfully.

Words should be used very carefully: when we don't have anything good to say, it's better to keep silent and not say anything at all. We need to be careful of everything we think and say because every thought and word is vibrating, creating, and supporting our reality. Improving our language and communication greatly improves our lives and relationships. When we are mindful of our thoughts and words, of how they make others feel, we can build healthier relationships. Thoughts and words create energy.

We all live on different levels of consciousness, and there will always be polarities in life. Negative and positive polarities are necessary, in the same way that the shadows allow us to see the light. We shouldn't try to deny negativity or shadows – they exist, and are part of the process of getting into the light. People who vibrate in negativity are not yet aware of the light or of what they are saying, thinking, or doing.

Many of us are not conscious of the existence of mental pollution. We are not aware that mental impurity is the real cause of our problems. Negative thinking and speech, such as lying, complaining or gossiping, takes us away from the pure infinite source that is available to us at every moment. Speaking too much is also a sign that we are out of balance. If we are not able to enjoy silence, we cannot be at peace with ourselves and others.

We do not want to continue to play the victims of this world, do we? We can step out of this victim role for our own freedom. We must take responsibility for our thoughts, words, and actions. We are free to choose what to think and how to react to any given event in our lives. Everything depends on us, not on others. We are not victims. When we leave the victim story behind, we step out of being a hostage of life and instead start being the creators of our lives. If we keep blaming other people for our pain, we are just delaying our own evolution and the possibility of our joy and happiness.

Now is a time of awakening, a time to connect to the source, to be mentally and physically healthy. You may think it might happen in the future... but life is happening now!

Just observe and ask:

How are my words impacting my life, other people's lives, and my environment? What kind of energy am I putting out into the world? Is it a real expression of my higher self?

We should use our mouths and words as instruments for the highest good so that we can effectively communicate and share love and gratitude with others. Our voices are instruments to be used in a peaceful and loving way, not as weapons with which to hurt others. Our voices should never be used to cause others suffering, but to alleviate their pain. We can heal our anger and transform our negative emotions. We can learn to use our voice as a pure expression of love and freedom.

There is a hidden manifestation power in words, and the more we think and say positive or negative things, the more we are directing that energy to manifest our experiences. Thinking is the first stage of manifesting. Then, words and action come. Consequently, if you refrain from having negative thoughts and words, and create the opposite force, with positive thoughts and words, you will begin to see how everything just gently flows in your favor.

When we shift polarities from negative to positive in our mind, our experiences will also shift for the better. When we shift our consciousness, we will be able to experience heaven on Earth. Even if the shadows and negativity still exist, we no longer play the role of the victim. We know that we are all creators, and we create our future with the power of our minds and hearts. With this knowledge, we can begin to heal ourselves and Mother Earth.

AFFIRMATIONS

American author Louise Hay had a tremendously difficult upbringing. She was raped at the age of five and had to run away from home when she was 16 because of the violent environment and abuse of her step-father. Then she became pregnant and had to make the difficult decision to give her baby up for adoption. Later in her adult life, she was diagnosed with cancer. She had all the reasons possible in this world to be a victim of life. But she did not take on this role. She decided to learn meditation, energy work, and healing; and by doing so she transformed herself and was able to cure her cancer.

Hay wrote her first book *You Can Heal Your Life* based on her own experiences and life story. This was written in a time when she thought people wouldn't be interested in this topic. She didn't even look for a publisher, she just decided she would print a few hundred copies for her students. Her book sold more than 34 million copies and has been translated into dozens of languages. By sharing her story, Hay was able to help millions of people around the world. Hay is an example of someone who had so much suffering in her life, but instead of letting it take over, she made the choice to learn and surrender to the spiritual dimension of herself. It was from her discovery of self-affirmations and self-talk that she was able to heal and to teach people the power of our thoughts and words.

Hay showed how repeating positive affirmations is like installing new programs in our brain. As a result of installing and updating our programs, it is possible to learn, practice, and eventually tune our mind to positive thinking. Using affirmations continuously helps us to let go of the negative thoughts that we may be used to thinking or hearing. By replacing them with positive affirmations, we activate certain areas of the brain that exude more love and beauty. We all have the capability to guide our minds and thoughts to positively help ourselves, the people around us and all the events in our lives.

I often ask myself, *Is it really possible to stop thinking?* Thinking is as involuntary as breathing is, but unlike the latter, it can easily become negative and destructive. Although we are aware of the mind's process, we can still become used to negative thinking to a point where it gets out of control and we become trapped by it. The mind is such a powerful vessel, but what happens when we don't use it properly? Oftentimes, it will start working against us, sometimes to the point where even our cells work against the body. Viruses may appear and start attacking the body, just like a hacker who installs a virus in a computer — it starts sabotaging itself.

If we just take the time to learn how to properly guide our mind, giving it direction and guiding it along the way, we can turn it into a powerful ally. Nevertheless, we tend to believe our thoughts aren't real or important, or we don't pay attention to them, but the truth is: our thoughts are creating our reality. Thinking of abundance can only bring you more abundance. Thinking of love and compassion can only bring the same experience. But don't forget, the same principle works in the negative direction as well.

What you think is what you become.

A strong mind keeps thinking in a positive direction—beauty, love, virtue, and determination—and the person that has such a mind will succeed. Subsequently, as we listen and repeat positive affirmations regularly as a practice, we create new patterns of thoughts, new pathways in our brain. A new energy will form and replace old, stagnant energy. As the mind repeats positivity intentionally, we are reprogramming ourselves, and a positive affirmation is installed inside our system. The lack of self-worth that was bugging the system before is replaced with self-love.

Once, I heard someone say, "I am passionate about infecting people with optimism." I loved it! Our affirmations are like slogans, a mantra that we intensively repeat inside our mind. When we do this, energy is created all through our bodies, which, ultimately, has the power to affect and inspire others. Inspiration is a light of beauty and wisdom. Use this light to help someone to grow, to change something that needs to be changed. This light and the power to sprout seeds is within us all. It's up to us to offer the soil and give water in our minds and hearts and to use its fullest potential. When the seeds fruit they provide nourishment for other people.

Ideas, thoughts, feelings, and affirmations are like seeds we spread around us. They will affect us in a positive or negative way. And remember, the nature of every seed is to grow and eventually give flowers and fruits, and spread more seeds. Positive thinking is a beautiful seed, that when nurtured with love, quickly grows and multiplies, reaching more and more people. Consequently, we are creating a better world. Take this wisdom inside of your being:

It is all in your mind, you are creating your experiences with the way you think. Change the way you think and you will change the outcome of your experiences.

Remind yourself that thinking negatively creates negative experiences, negative emotions and negative relationships in your life. The path we take and the way we think will always lead us somewhere. We need to know where we are going with our thinking, and in which direction we want to lead our mind. Everything in this world has cause and effect; it is a very basic law of nature. When we think optimistically, when we can laugh at our challenges and smile at life, we will reap a better outcome. It is that simple. Remember that the beauty of life is not in reaching our final destination but in enjoying the exhilarating journey. It is all about smiling, enjoying the beauty of nature, the adventures along the way, all the people we meet, and every experience we have.

Into Practice

I am sharing here some very simple affirmations I have been using for many years that work well for me. I believe they can bring enormous benefits to anyone who starts doing this practice regularly. But remember: affirmations are like training: you get stronger and stronger with practice. For affirmations to work you need to guide your thinking in the direction you want to reach.

If I did not have a strong and determined mind I could not have done all I have so far. For that I have been exercising and training my mind for the challenges of life, relationships, work, etc.

Just as you can train your body, you can also train your mind to get stronger.

What I regularly do is: I just stop, close my eyes, breathe and say to myself "breathing in, I know I am breathing in, breathing out, I know I am breathing out", and I smile. Simple as that. I repeat it a few times, breathing in, breathing out. I acknowledge my breath and come back to the present moment; it helps me to become conscious of my breath, this life force, this prana energy within us. I then affirm: "I have arrived, I am home... here and now, in this present moment, in each and every breath." For me, it is a good reminder of how precious it is to live in the present moment, which is all that we truly have. It brings me into presence, body and mind united. I am affirming that I am aware of my breath and that I am choosing to live in the present moment.

As I go forward, I then use affirmations of health and gratitude for each part of my body. Starting from the feet and going up part by part, I scan my body, saying thank you for each organ and gland, all systems, bones, muscles and veins, and all senses and for everything. And then I affirm gratitude for all other areas of my life; friends, family, ancestors, all masters, angels and beloved teachers... to Mother Earth and all the elements that nourish us.

I affirm gratitude for everything that comes to my mind during that day and that moment. I affirm gratitude even for all the challenges and difficult times, seeing them as opportunities for growth. I affirm pure love for this divine energy. And I repeat "I love you" to this divine energy. I affirm that I know divine energy can hear me and I am going deeper and deeper into my heart, focusing my mind like a laser and allowing pure love to enter my body, where love is the healing energy. I affirm, "I trust the universe."

In humbleness, I also affirm that I am sorry and I ask for forgiveness, not only for myself but for our ancestors and all humanity, and even for the things that I do not understand. I affirm that in the infinitude of this universe, I know all is perfect, whole and complete. That in the center of my heart there is an infinite source of love, like a pure source of water that comes from the earth, and I allow this love to fill my whole being, my spirit, my mind, my consciousness, all parts of me, in all directions.

I affirm that I know this source is endless and is right inside of me; I know I can always access this infinite source and that the more love I give, the more love I have to give because the source is endless. I affirm that all is well and I keep repeating "I love you" and "thank you" to this divine energy. Basically, I combine affirmations with the meditation technique of the Ho'oponopono, which I will dedicate an entire chapter to later in the book.

I have affirmed all these sentences for many years. Most recently I affirm that I am open to prosperity and the abundance of the universe, and that all that comes to my hand will be used not only for my highest good but to share with others and create beautiful projects to help other living beings, animals, plants and minerals.

You too can take a piece of paper and start to make your affirmations. Later, it will become more and more natural and these affirmations will become part of your daily life. Note that all our thinking and the words we speak are affirmations all the time that we are saying to ourselves and to others.

Many times, if my mind was foggy or if I had to do any housework, such as cleaning or cooking (which I did a lot while living in Switzerland), I would often listen to Louise Hay's self-healing affirmations that I had downloaded from YouTube. I would also do this regularly before falling asleep.

I believe the last one or two hours before we sleep are very important for our quality of sleep, which greatly affects our life. It is the time we turn our mind off, and synchronize to the frequency we want to match during the night. Instead of watching television or using the phone, looking at social media and messages, I try to use this special time to synchronize myself and have only beautiful and positive information going through my system. In the same way, the first one or two hours in the morning are very precious for setting the quality of our days. These are the best times to practice affirmations and meditation. If I can not start my day with yoga or with a good smile, I start with good music and some affirmations. I work on myself when I feel I need upliftment. I also listen to Plum Village songs and Dharma talks. This always helps uplift me when I need more strength for my upcoming tasks or while working at home.

Anyway, the most important thing for me is to do everything with love, no matter what, and to combine my daily tasks and activities with my inner work. I do not believe the inner and outer can ever be separated. Even if I am cleaning the floor, I can use it as an opportunity to practice mindfulness and do it with love. In situations where the task is very hard, I will affirm and repeat: "I am sorry, please forgive me," to the divine energy. And I affirm: "I trust every situation is for my highest good." I speak to divine energy, I feel it cleaning me from the inside.

Mind Training

With all that being said, we can start training ourselves.

Start training your mind like you'd train to run a marathon.

Like a marathon runner who needs to train before running 42 kilometers, any person who wants to be happier can train their mind. With mental training, we nourish ourselves with happiness, benevolence, attention, emotional balance, and resilience. So, if we put them all together, we can say that happiness is a competence that can be acquired. In this regard, we can train our mind to be happier. All of those seeds are available for us, waiting to be watered inside our hearts.

> *"Start by thinking happy thoughts for 10 to 20 minutes a day. Typically when we experience feelings of happiness and love, it's fleeting and then something else happens, and we move on to the next thought. Instead, concentrate on not letting your mind get distracted, and keep focused on the positive emotions for the next stretch of time. If you do that training every day, even just two weeks later you can feel positive mental results."*
>
> *Matthieu Ricard*

The practice of awareness happens through observation of the mind; by bringing attention to the present moment and seeing what is going on inside of ourselves. First, we must observe what is going on in our operational system. Although we are aware of the mind's process, we can still become trapped by it. The mind is such a powerful vessel, but what happens when we don't use it properly? Often, it will start working against us, sometimes to the point where even our cells work against the body. Viruses may appear and start attacking the body, just like a hacker who installs a virus in a computer so that it starts sabotaging itself.

I am regularly aware of my body, my mind, my feelings, and my consciousness, in order to see how well they are functioning. I am human and I make mistakes, but I am able to forgive myself because I know none of us is perfect. We learn from our mistakes, from falling and standing back up again. Sometimes we fall down, and it can often take a while until we are able to stand up again, but it is all part of the learning process.

The most important thing is that we recognize our mistakes and learn from them. Understand the message life is giving you so that you don't repeat the same mistakes. Life is a spiritual journey and we only truly learn when we experience and make mistakes. No matter what happens, I am able to forgive myself because I am only a human being. Although we have an incredible operating system and can experience the highest states of being—love and compassion—we need to be patient with ourselves in this process.

You can be trapped in the mind for many days, months, or even years, but eventually, you will wake up to the truth. It is all about understanding the cycles of life and following the path of liberation, non-attachment, freedom, and joy. We do not need to continue cycles of pain and suffering, we have had enough. Suffering is an illusion created by the mind. The mind becomes stuck the longer we are away from nature and from our own nature. The mind can take us in many different directions, causing our energy levels to decrease, and if we don't go into nature enough, and feel the earth in us, we start to forget. The mind forgets very easily.

I recall the five precepts of Buddhism to keep us on track:

Do not kill.

Do not lie.

Do not steal.

Do not engage yourself in any dishonest sexual relationship.

Do not use alcohol and drugs.

These are not simply Buddhist precepts but universal and timeless principles for life.

This is a path of liberation. The five precepts are clearly and simply laid out, and by following this path, we can turn suffering into freedom, and tune into the frequency of understanding, love and compassion.

You have everything you need to be a happy and fulfilled person.

Taking Time to Enjoy Work & Nature

What happens when we feel overwhelmed? When we feel we have so much to do? When time seems to go by so quickly that we cannot do everything we would like to do? There are times when the days just go on and on like this, and you just want to escape, to be free of all these worries and responsibilities. But you feel trapped in your work. You just want to go back to that pure state of mind, to your inner child, but you have become an adult, and other people now depend on you.

What should you do when you are feeling overwhelmed?

This is when we need to go back to our breath and take refuge in spiritual teachings. Only when we look deeply into our own nature we can remember. The world is out there just waiting for us but we have been closing ourselves off in a box and not deeply questioning what we have been doing. Many of us have been turning on the TV or our cell phones and forgetting everything about true life.

We might ask ourselves, "What is the meaning of my work?"

We do not just want a means to an end; we want to know that what we are doing day-to-day serves a wider purpose. We want to feel part of something meaningful.

There's a famous anecdote about the cleaner at NASA who, when asked by JFK what his role was, replied that he was helping to put a man on the moon.

Without a clear purpose in mind, anything we spend hours actioning can, unsurprisingly, start to feel meaningless. But it all happens in the mind. When we understand our tasks within the context of something bigger, they quickly gain meaning.

It's our human nature to seek meaning and purpose in everyday life. Psychiatrist Viktor Frankl, author of *Man's Search for Meaning* says that the search for meaning is the "primary, intrinsic motivation of human beings." Feeling appreciated alongside a sense of belonging is extremely important in the workplace to help you find purpose in your role.

Research shows that people are more productive, creative and engaged when they feel like their work is contributing to a wider goal. All this makes for a healthier, happier, more productive person. This encompasses more than just progression and financial gain.

We all want to feel part of a wider mission. We can have a strong set of values in what we choose to work on. As we understand our clear purpose, we can write down reminders and lovingly hang them up on the walls of our home or office, giving ourselves and anyone who comes around a snapshot of what we're working towards and what we stand for. These are simple gestures, but help put everyday tasks into perspective, making them understood in terms of our larger purpose and, ultimately, bestowing them with meaning.

Work becomes more meaningful when we get to see the fruits of our labour. Witnessing and appreciating the impact our work has on the world at large can be hugely rewarding. But the idea of a tangible impact doesn't just relate to any specific job, such as charity workers helping the homeless, doctors treating sick patients or scientists developing cures for life-threatening illnesses. A sense of tangible impact can relate to any profession, whether a chef who is preparing a healthy meal, a coder working on a new app or an architect building a new home; we all can make people's lives better. Everyone can get to see and celebrate the impact their work is having.

Indeed, we can measure our success by the benefit we bring to those we affect. Once again, this doesn't mean only customers, but everyone that works with us; our team and also our community. We help each person become the best version of themselves, both in and outside our workplace.

There's no single way of imbuing work with meaning. We all find meaning in different places. For many, it's the feeling of contributing to a wider purpose, a purpose they believe in. For others, it's seeing the impact their work is having, seeing their efforts coming into fruition in the real world. And for others still, it's developing themselves, building on their own knowledge base and skillset.

Overall, our work can be a space for development and growth. With this in mind, believe that you can choose the work you wish to have, and the life you would like to live. And that you too can make your choices based on love.

The balance between our work and personal life is very important. If we are working overtime, our personal life will be neglected. Aside from work, we must start by making more free space to clean up our limitations, worries, and anxieties. To be able to breathe deeply and look at the beauty that surrounds us. It is crucial that you also have time to enjoy life otherwise you will lose your sense of being. Are you ready to liberate yourself? To get out of the box? To trust yourself and to trust life?

Indeed, all of life's challenges are just making us stronger and stronger. We know that there are cycles in life; observe and pass through them without getting attached or caught up in the mistakes. But do not make the same mistakes again, because time is precious.

We should not underestimate the power of nature to renew us. Every time you need help, go to nature, and connect with it by looking deeply at it. When you do this, you will be able to understand things more clearly because nature is the best teacher. When you don't take the time to connect with nature, your vision becomes clouded. Open your heart and your eyes to Mother Earth and reconnect with the beauty of life.

In this way, you will allow peace to reside inside you. Be at peace with your own roots so that storms do not destroy you anymore. Learn from nature, and if you need help, ask for it. Nature might help you more than you ever imagined, because you just need silence to reach peace. Quiet down, calm down and relax your mind in order to be able to feel the calming energy of nature.

Please Mother Earth, help me!

Whenever I can, I go to nature to remind myself of the peace and beauty that is in every moment. We must reconnect with nature inside of us. We can merely open our eyes to recognize beauty. And when we open our hearts and minds, we can truly see it everywhere. I can go deep with my roots in this inner peace because I know the Universe is and will always support me. Also, I understand that to reconnect with my true self I need less talking and more action. In this way, I can become a pure channel, letting the vitality of life course through me.

When was the last time you were in deep silence with nature, just feeling the moment in each step and each breath you took?

Maybe this is what you need now: to step away from your responsibilities, challenges, or objectives. Just take this time for yourself and allow nature to recharge your batteries. Just recharge and be with yourself in silence. Actually, not only with yourself but with the trees, the birds, the sky, the animals and the fresh air. Feel the present moment unfolding in each step and each breath. Now is the time to empty yourself, relax and enjoy this precious life that has been given to you!

Smile, You Are Alive!

We have an energy field around our bodies. When we shine, our energy field radiates, and it reflects on the people living around us. As we become aware of energy, vibration, sound and frequency, we start to return to our original and natural state of being: love. This movement happens from the inside out, and it can be very easy if we choose to make it simple or it can be very difficult if we prefer to make it complicated.

Be aware of how you breathe, of how you walk, think, talk, and act. Remember to always smile, give a great laugh about this cosmic joke! If you have lost your smile, go and get it back! Go and look for the flowers, and ask them, "Please, can you give me back my smile?" By looking deeply into the flowers, you will see how they smile back at you. Connect to them and see yourself smiling again.

Remember, your smile is like a flower, and every time you smile it is like you are giving a flower to someone.

When we look deeply, we can see that sacredness is everywhere in nature. Observe nature; all the answers to life are there. To be able to make fruits, the tree must give flowers first. If you want to manifest your dreams in this reality, you must give lots of smiles. There is no other way.

As you smile more and more, the flower eventually transforms into a fruit. It's very attractive, beautiful, and pleasant to see. Think how pleasant it is to be around people who are bright, smiling and laughing most of the time. Being joyful is an understanding that the Universe loves good humor.

If you take everything so seriously, not smiling and laughing, if you have lost your enthusiasm and are not playful with life, you are blocking the energy flow and preventing your dreams from coming true. Give yourself a little practice right now. Bring this inner smile to your lips, and let yourself shine!

Be aware that being playful and joyful do not mean not to take on responsibility for things. It means mostly to be and to make life more pleasant for ourselves and for others. Think about how pleasant it is to have people with beautiful smiles, without stress, next to you. With a smile you can help everything become easier and more relaxed. In fact, we can be more productive and fruitful.

If you want to manifest dreams, you must find ways of laughing and smiling, of being cheerful with life. Give more flowers and give more smiles to people. Smile at yourself, smile at life!

6. SEEDS OF DREAMS

The imaginary and the real might seem like two different worlds. Now, I will dive into the world of dreams, where we will see how both the real and the imaginary are intricately connected. In a way, it is like the world of the person who could see different dimensions but could not hold it and got lost, losing control of the mind and disconnecting from reality. The imaginary goes beyond any logic. My work here is to show that both worlds exist and that there is a bridge between them.

We are inside this magic, the wonders of life and dreams are available for us all the time; we can always go there. We are inside the dream of our own cosmic existence. It is so big that we can only dream its immensity.

Understanding Dreams

Dreams remain a mystery for scientists and all of humankind. In the usual sense, dreams refer to a series of thoughts, images, or emotions that occur during sleep. But they go far beyond this. In my search for a better definition, I found the experience of waking life having the characteristics of a dream, such as a visionary creation of the imagination. Indeed, a dream, for our purposes, has the following elements: a DAYDREAM: an object or idea seen in a dreamlike state; A VISION: something notable for its beauty, excellence, or enjoyable quality; a strongly desired goal or purpose and/or something that fully satisfies a wish. And an IDEAL.

The most important thing here is to understand that we can experience awakened dream states naturally, dreams are not limited to sleep. Although the dreams we have during our sleep many times contain insights and important messages for the soul, it is possible for us to access these realms without sleep.

I have been leading a life of dreams and reality—between the real and the imaginary—building a bridge between these two worlds. Anyway, for me, there is not really a separation. "Real" and "imaginary" are only concepts. When we let go of that, we realize that one exists only because the other exists. And so it is with all apparent dualities. As I grow older, I understand more and more that even the polarities of things we call negative or positive are fundamental to each other's existence. It is all an integrated existence.

Now, we are in the middle of the cake. This is very intimate. In this chapter, I am about to share my most secret dreams with you. One might think I am crazy, but do I care?

The rainbow is a friend of mine. You can be a friend of a frog or a snake, just as you can be a friend of the rainbow or a tiny flower. You can have a special relationship with anything you wish when you connect from your heart. Just by writing this book I am establishing a relationship with you. It is a relationship grounded in love. I believe love is what we are all made of, and just as all rivers lead to the ocean, we too will arrive at the ocean of infinite love sooner or later. We are in a process of disappearing and unifying with something bigger, much bigger than ourselves. A sense of wholeness and collectivism is emerging on our planet. Part of me knows I am still a person, but I am also aware that I am connected to the rest of humanity, to all living beings and creatures, and to my true nature—the cosmic reality.

It is with humility that I offer you this chapter, to go beyond the sense of "I" and become a unified “we”. It is not I AM, but WE ARE. Somehow, when I think “I am,” I feel small, but when I think “we are,” I feel something much greater. Picture birds, for example. One single bird, when flying alone, needs a lot of energy. But when a group of birds fly together in a V formation they have the power to travel greater distances. This is exactly what happens when we unify forces. The strength of collectivism dwarfs the power of individuality. A singular twig can be snapped in two with little pressure, but a bundle of sticks keep its form even when faced with immense pressure.

By sharing our stories and experiences, we reinforce this sense of unity. This is amazing because it gives us so many possibilities, and we can learn in a myriad of ways. We can use the example of other people’s experiences for our highest purposes. It might be through joy and happiness or pain and suffering, but as intelligent beings, we do not need to repeat the same mistakes anymore. We open ourselves to new ways of understanding the world and understanding our existence. Seeing from another’s perspective allows us to comprehend things in different ways. Through this process, we have the possibility of changing ourselves and creating a better life on our beloved planet. We unify our experiences into one collective power.

This is an invitation to fly together on a journey to the heart where we will fly further than we could ever have imagined. Without a doubt, this is exactly what we need: to unify our forces with this universal power, and learn how to use it in order to transform our reality and heal ourselves and Mother Earth. Then each of us, together, can contribute on a collective level to uplift the collective consciousness by spreading this loving energy.

It does not matter where you are; there is no distance, time or space separating us in the realms of dreams. Now, let us go on this journey together, to dream our deepest and most beautiful dreams, and to contribute to a better life on this planet. We can make it happen!

I have many secret stories about the rainbow; many of them crazy and magical. But in this first book, I will share just two beautiful rainbow stories with you. Any more would be too much in one dose. I promise I will tell you more in the future. A second book baby is on its way. This time, I will keep the focus on inner gardening, planting seeds. I could write an entire book about dreams, but I must make the bridge. I must give you strong foundations. If we take on too much at once, we can bust the energy and break down. Now, let's increase the energy to fly higher and higher, and ascend on the wings of dreams!

How to Dream

Awakened dreaming starts with TRUST. Trust this divine intelligence that governs life. Many of us have forgotten how to dream as we used to when we were innocent little children. Maybe we think we are too old to dream again or might even be afraid to live in an awakened dream state. We might doubt we can experience life becoming pure magic again.

Remembering how to dream is the first step in bringing magic back into our lives. We can start finally living our dreams and learn to recognize how the Universe is always supporting us.

Be sure to guide your life in the direction of your dreams. And call to mind the following:

1. Remind yourself how to dream again. The little child we once were is inside all of us. Start laughing and being playful!
2. Every step you take is precious. Take action to live out your highest dreams. Be ready! Trust.
3. Stay on track and follow the heart. Let love guide you. Love is the healing energy.

There are no limits to our dreams because we are both the dream and the dreamer at the same time. Dreaming is the essence of consciousness because consciousness is a dream in itself. Once, whilst meditating during a workshop in Slovenia, I had a vision that there were infinite beings within me that were communicating and working together as a close-knit community. In a dreamlike state, I could feel my consciousness tapping into the frequencies of my cells, and they seemed to respond to this. It was as if my cells were pleased that I was acknowledging them in such a fine way. Going further, it was not only my cells but all the micro-organisms that lived within my body.

In this dream, I saw Earth as a pupil within the eye of a giant being. This eye contained flowing, multicolored dimensions of the Universe, almost like I had entered a different dimension of reality. When I described this experience to a few others in the workshop, some of them looked at me as if I had taken magic mushrooms. They could not believe I wasn't on any kind of psychedelic drug.

As a matter of fact, our consciousness has the capacity to take us into the fractal and foreign realms of reality that seem only accessible by taking strong psycho-active substances. These awakenings can happen in a natural way when we are ready, but some people try to open their third eye and break open the door to other dimensions through the use of Psilocybin Mushrooms, DMT, LSD, etc.

> *Magical experiences are happening now and in every moment; it is all about perception.*

Once, I was lying in a hammock, staring at the sunset over a beautiful oceanic landscape and I thought: *How come people cannot see the magic that is happening all around us at every single moment?* Many people take drugs to try to see other realms of reality, when there is already so much to see here. Many of us are walking as if we are blind and this is because we have not awakened to what is happening in each moment, in the NOW. Most of us are not able to enjoy what we already have because we do not realize that we already have everything we need!

Once, in another dream, I could see and feel everything that was under my skin: my bones, blood, muscles and veins. For many months afterwards, I would often see people without skin. This might seem scary for some, but for me it was amazing and very interesting to be awake to the truth under our skin. To be able to see not only the reality under our clothes, but our skin. This simple awareness made me remember the magic I witnessed that day in the hammock. If we truly look inside ourselves, we can see the magic of our own nature, our body and everything around us. Simply looking inside or listening to the sounds of birds, water, wind, and music is already opening up to magic; it is all there, simply everywhere, just waiting to be seen.

You can undergo powerful, transformative experiences in a purely natural state with the correct setting and by trusting and surrendering to this divine energy.

Yogis have also known for generations that these dimensions are accessible through meditation. Forcing these experiences by taking hallucinogens might cause false electrical currents to surge through the body, resulting in a psychotic break. This happens when the body has too much energy from other realms, and it reaches a burnout stage. One needs to cultivate a higher threshold of energy over time to gracefully handle these experiences and retain equilibrium. A light bulb can only handle a certain amount of electricity before its filaments burst, but if you can somehow acclimatize this bulb into generating a larger energy capacity, it will shine brighter than ever before.

Many times during my meditations, I would visualize myself floating within the Universe, looking at Mother Earth with an overflow of love inside of me. I would have tears of joy running down my face, like an ocean of love that I could not keep inside. It was powerful and fragile at the same time, just a flood of love and emotions.

What is so interesting is how there are so many layers of dreams. One dream is inside another dream, that is inside another dream. It seems that it is never-ending! All my experiences of dreams in this life interact with both the imaginary and the reality. At the same time I am dreaming, I am also living the dream as a reality—an awakening is happening every day! Are you dreaming? Think about it and ask yourself:

What is my dream now? What is it that my soul wants to experience?

I have different kinds of dreams. My biggest dream is not an individual dream, but a collective one. My biggest dream is a dream of a humanity of compassion. I dream of a better future for humanity, that we will wake up to love and drop the masks of the ego, our illusions of the self, to live a life of authenticity, reconnected with nature. I dream that we as humanity will one day be able to see the sacredness of life within us, leading us, in this way, to heal Mother Earth and ourselves.

What drives my dreams is not pleasure but freedom. The same freedom I felt flying high above the clouds, with my paragliding wings one day, astonished by the beauty, feeling that sense of adventure and aliveness. Adventures might have risks, but fears cannot stop us from fulfilling our dreams. We must trust the Universe and this divine intelligence.

In the end, it is love that remains and matters the most.

I have both small and big dreams. I also dream of creating a bigger sustainable community where people can connect deeply with nature, with themselves and with one another. And where we can appreciate the stars and practice the Dharma, a pure way of life, together. I dream and believe in a future of more and more self-sustainable communities being created around Earth, and that wonderful people are supporting them and making it happen.

Experience expands consciousness and visions. We can only share what we already have. We need to be full of love ourselves in order to share love with others. We need to be full of freedom in order to share freedom with others. We have to expand our consciousness so we can help others expand their own consciousness. I am ready to expand the community, because I already see it within me.

Right now, our dreams might seem very far away. But our perception is what is creating our reality. Remember, life is a dream, and we shift from one dream of reality to another dream of reality. Different dreams, different lives, different experiences. There are many different realities inside one another, like levels of consciousness. I have been talking about the reality that I have been experiencing; it only appears to be mine, but every other reality is part of ONE big dream. Life embraces us all, and in the end, all dissolves, disappears and transforms. By the time we die, everything of this body will be gone; just a memory stored in consciousness, somewhere in the Universe.

When we recognize our mortality, we lose our attachments. We become grateful for each day life gives us, and every moment. We are the dreamers, living the dreams, but are not attached to any of them. And we are awakening! We enjoy living in the NOW, in this present moment! And so, we learn how to live and to dream, and most of all, how to love. Remember to be truly grateful for everything, for every blessing and suffering. Gratitude is the vibration fulfilling our dreams. Gratitude is the key to living a happy and satisfied life. Let us now go into some dreams—awakened dream states!

Thank you, thank you, thank you to the Universe!

RAINBOW DREAMS

Now I am getting into the cake. I have such a love story with the rainbow. I love rainbows themselves as much as I love the consciousness, perception, and feelings that they bring. This is a strange and funny love story. In this story, dreams and reality are blended together. This widens the spectrum of our consciousness and enables us to regard this new perception of love. This story is not only an idea, but also a concrete manifestation and experience of this world.

Sometimes we use a word or an image to represent our feelings. The rainbow, like many things, can be seen as a symbol, a representative of dreams. For me, when the rainbow appears, it serves as a reminder of what I might have forgotten, and, thus, gives me a chance to improve my reality and to dream. We are here to evolve, to learn, and to become better human beings. When we go down that path, everything starts to change. Wonders are unleashed, and we can tap into the most powerful energy that exists: love. We all have this energy inside of us, and large amounts of it are stored and waiting to be activated. We can create higher amounts of power and energy in ourselves when we learn how to activate love, tuning and harmonizing heart and mind.

We might have never learned to do this in school, society, or even in our families. So we have to make our own evolutionary path until we arrive to see our wholeness and our holiness. Here, we go beyond what is visible to our eyes. Certainly, there is a spectrum of colors and consciousness inside each one of us. Just like a rainbow is a spectrum full of colors.

Therefore, consider rainbows as animated creatures, with their colors, beauty, hopes and dreams. Rainbows will do everything for you when you get to know their power. Inspiration, beauty, poetry; they all come from the soul and from dreams. You might wonder –or still not understand. What am I talking about? What is this story about rainbows, colors, magic, beauty, and dreams? Some people think that life is just full of problems, misery and tragedy. So, what is the truth?

Rainbows make us pause and admire them, appreciating the magic of such precious moments. They are here to bring us together, and they do this with surprises, beauty and infinite love. This story is not mine; it has a life of its own. Maybe it never was mine at all, it just came through me as a kind of love contribution from Mother Earth to help us heal ourselves and our planet. Rainbows are with me, and they always will be, because unlimited love binds us together. I feel we are all connected through a higher love from the same mother and father, and living in the same home, this spaceship called Earth.

My relationship with the rainbow started a long time ago, maybe before I can even remember. But when I first went to India, I was crying one night in total disappointment with God and human beings. I felt that humans everywhere were cruel and messed up, and so I wrote a small letter to God. This letter was a kind of prayer, but in the form of very personal conversation.

That night I gave up my dreams of a loving and spiritual world. I had gone to India with an open heart. I was supposed to go to a spiritual retreat and all I found was people fighting for power. Since the founder of the organization had passed away, the monks had been fighting for control of the organization. I saw so much misery and poverty not only in India, but also in so many wealthy people in different countries. Everywhere in the world—even in an ashram. Traditionally, an **ashram** (Sanskrit word) is a spiritual hermitage or a monastery, somewhere I thought would be a most sacred place.

"The rainbow doesn't exist," I cried, tears rolling down my face. "And so, Father, the rainbow doesn't really exist? It is all a big illusion of mine, isn't it? I am so sorry... I was mistaken, just a dream about the rainbow... about beauty, love, and spirituality. Maybe human beings are just so lost, and there is nothing real out there, or anything I can do. It was all my mistake, my illusion."

And that was it, the only thing I could write on the blank page in front of me.

I fell asleep with tears in my eyes and the notebook opened next to me. But the Universe heard my questions and answered the very next morning. Some of the most incredible experiences were about to happen in my life.

The next morning, I went outside, and the first thing I saw was a paraglider flying in the sky, with the green forests and the Himalayas in the background. My heart began pulsating so fast like an alarm was going off. I felt a strong urge to go to the paraglider. Somehow I had to fly! And so I dropped my toothbrush from the balcony of the little guest house, put my slippers on and started running, my hair whipping in the wind and fire in my heart. I had to get there fast. I was in a rush, given I had only a few minutes to find the place where the glider was going to land. I knew I couldn't miss it—it felt like the most important thing in my life at that moment.

I rented a bicycle and rode by a big, beautiful lake, passing many buffalos on the way, but that was a dead end, so I went back and took another road to reach the other side where the landing area was. A few minutes later, I finally reached the landing spot. By the time I got there, the pilot was already walking with the glider on his back, and with a woman passenger nearby. I stopped my bicycle a few meters away and kept watching him as he walked in my direction. As he came closer to me, it was like I could see his aura, bright and shining. I have always believed in energy and had recently read the book *The Celestine Prophecy*, by James Redfield, which I loved and which had raised my awareness on the subject. This moment reminded me of the things I had read. With each step, the aura of this handsome young man radiated stronger. I was taken aback by such a strong presence.

Finally, as he came closer, I built up the courage to talk to him. I told him that I had been traveling in India, that I used to be a pilot in Brazil, that I was feeling very sad for a few different reasons and I would love to fly. I told him that flying was my passion but as it was not the purpose of my travel, I had not brought my wings. I asked him if he had wings for rent. He said no, but that as he was opening a flight school in Nepal, he would be happy to take me on a flight with him the very next day. Somehow, from the moment we met—even though we had only exchanged a few words—I already knew he was going to be the man of my life.

The next day, we went flying, and I got an answer from the Universe in a completely unexpected way. To reach the take-off site, we took a two-hour drive and a half-hour walk. On the way there, I was sitting on the rooftop of the Jeep on top of big bags of paragliding wings, appreciating the incredible views of the Himalayas with a few other pilots who were joining the expedition. By the time we were preparing our equipment, I was a bit nervous and excited, and as our bodies got closer when we connected our harnesses, I could already feel a warmth inside me. After taking off from 1,000 meters we quickly reached 3,500 meters, flying among the clouds and the eagles. I could sense the powerful presence of this God of the sky, this young strong man, feeling half bird and half human. It was just the two of us up there, and we were literally above the clouds. Suddenly, something magical happened. With the clouds below and the sun above us, the difference of the temperature and humidity of the clouds produced a circular rainbow, and inside the rainbow we could see our shadows! The circular rainbow is a rare phenomenon I had seen before while flying, but I could never have imagined it might appear the very next day after my question.

It was incredibly magical. The Universe had responded in such an overwhelming way, and I was in total shock and surprise. I couldn't have expected an answer so fast and beautiful. I felt like I had been slapped in the face by the wings of an angel. Internally I was exclaiming, "Oh Father, your power is infinite. Yes, I understand now. The rainbow does exist! I will never doubt it again."

There might be darkness in the world, but there is also light. I knew this was the Universe answering my cries for help, and it was so clear. Life gives us answers all the time, and in many ways, but it is up to us to see or hear them. The Universe gave me not only an answer, but had also brought me the man I would spend my life with. David was his name, and he is the gentlest, sweetest, most beautiful, courageous and generous man I could ever have asked for. For him I would go to the moon if I had to. Over the following years we would travel to some of the most remote areas in Nepal and India. Together, we would live in Nepal for 11 years, have two children, and travel the world. We have created a beautiful story together, living different kinds of lifestyles in different parts of the planet, and supporting each other in every moment.

This rainbow story was already too beautiful to be real and could have just stopped there, but this was just the beginning. My love story with rainbows would keep going deeper and deeper. Afterwards, rainbows would keep showing up in real and awakened dreams. Life is made of experiences, not theories. We get to experience this truth, we live it to the fullest, love it to the fullest, and we do the best we can. We just need to open our wings and dream the most beautiful things we can. In this process, we will learn just how wonderful Earth is. I am a witness to the power of dreams.

In the dream, everything is possible.

Inside the Rainbow

One day, the sky became dark and a big summer storm arrived. While rain poured down, I ran to the lake to take a swim in pure delight and to connect with the elements. I could hear the thunder and see the giant strikes of lightning in the distance. The Himalayas were hidden behind the clouds, and the rain became so heavy that all I could see were raindrops falling from the sky. My insides smiled with every breath, and the rain became tears of joy that mixed with love from the Earth, just like when you smile and cry at the same time.

I felt the heavy drops of rain as blessings falling from the sky, as I appreciated the warm water of the lake and the power of nature—the thunder did not scare me. Something very mysterious and incredible happened to me that day. Something that would be sealed in my memory for the rest of my life on this Earth. Something that would blow my mind beyond my most imaginable dreams.

Suddenly, as the rain stopped and peace returned to the sky, a magnificent rainbow appeared in front of me, with all the magical colors one could only dream of. It was coming all the way from the distant mountain, and it was so close to me! It was a moment of astonishment and extreme beauty. The rainbow was so near, it was an incredible miracle. I could not believe my eyes! It was my dream rainbow!

I kept swimming in excitement, getting closer and closer to it. Again, my heart was pulsating so fast and with so much emotion. I arrived at the inside of the magnificent rainbow in the middle of the lake, in an explosion of love and joy! It was like a strong current of electricity was circulating throughout my whole body. All my cells were having a kind of "super rainbow activation." There were no inner thoughts, just the feeling of total presence. I could feel the rays of the sun and the gentle drops of water in the air. My identity disappeared, I was nothing and everything, and all that was left was the pure feeling of love in my heart.

Reality and dreams were happening at the same time. I was in a dream beyond my imagination. Eternity was showing its face and Mother Earth was smiling at me, and I was feeling her presence radiating inside of me. Tears of joy and gratitude rolled down my face, mixing with the water of the lake. In that moment, I became the lake, the rainbow, the sky, the mountains of the Himalayas and everything that exists!

With a sweet tone I whispered to the rainbow, "Oh my dear, here you are! I love you so much! Thank you so much for being here!" Yes, wonders of life, it had happened! I was inside the rainbow!

After this experience, I felt an explosive wave of love ripple through me. It's funny to see how this wave has grown and become stronger and more powerful with time. A few minutes inside a rainbow will last forever in the blueprint of my soul; it was almost as if I had been transported to another dimension. The more we are able to see beauty, the more our heart vibrates full of joy and happiness.

This rainbow story could have finished there. And it would be so beautiful, like a fairy-tale. But it did not end. For my good fortune, the rainbow is always coming back again and again, bringing important messages. I give thanks to the dreams, to the rainbow and to our universal rainbow family, that includes all minerals, plants, animals, living beings and creatures of our beloved Earth.

Reflections of the Rainbow

For me, the rainbow is the symbol of the dream. Every time I see a rainbow, I am touched by its beauty. I know of its impermanence, as it appears for only a few minutes before it vanishes. Even though some of us may not be aware of it, witnessing the rainbow becomes part of us; stored in our brain as a memory, consciously or not. Despite only appearing for a couple of minutes, rainbows paint a portion of the sky and leave us with a powerful feeling. But when we look again, they are already gone!

It is only a matter of time before rainbows disappear, just like our own life. Eventually, we will die; we should never forget that or be afraid to speak about it. Ultimately, if we remember it every day, we'll be able to live life with much more gratitude and appreciation. The vision of the rainbow, with its full spectrum of colors, has the power to clean our energy and expand our awareness, by waking up the beauty that lies inside us. The rainbow brings us the message of the beauty, and the impermanence, of the visible and invisible world.

We can keep feelings alive and cultivate them as we wish, such as gardeners do with their seeds. We prepare the soil and cultivate the seeds we want to grow and keep alive. In the same way, we can also cultivate dreams. As we learn to cultivate beautiful thoughts and feelings, we prepare the soil from the inside, blossoming in the grace of our dreams.

Remember, the Universe is always responding to our dreams and what we focus our attention on. "What you look at is what you become," says the old wisdom.

If there are no limits to our dreams, why do so many people only dream of material and selfish things? Can we dream not only for ourselves but for all living beings and the whole Universe? Are you ready for expansion? Do you want to stay narrow-minded and see the world with only one color? Or do you want to experience the wholeness of the rainbow with its full spectrum of colors? Everything starts off as a dream, but then we step into action, and thereupon we start to experience the magic.

I have experienced many dreams in this lifetime, and this is why this book is happening now. I see more people wanting to experience life and dreams too. For this reason, my heart tells me to share with you everything I know about dreams, magic and rainbows. Allow yourself to dream consciously, to be awake and able to dream, to embody the dream. As we connect with the Universe and with this divine energy that supports us in our existence, we can experience our most beautiful dreams!

Ingredients to Experience Dreams

Experiencing dreams as reality doesn't happen solely in the mind, but happens in combination with the heart, the gut, and in reconnection with Mother Earth. It happens when we are not afraid; we trust this divine intelligence and so we make ourselves ready. In doing so, we increase our vibrational frequency.

As we increase our vibration, we will change the collective vibration on our planet. We will feel our divinity in its full potential, becoming "human rainbow beings"; those who can smile and make decisions based on love and compassion, reflecting the full spectrum of colors. As we increase our frequency, we simultaneously increase the frequency of our environment. Love's high frequency sends healing vibrations all around us.

I believe there are three basic ingredients necessary to experience dreams as reality:

1. Smile at life and laugh as much as possible;
2. Shift into love and make all your decisions based on love;
3. Be ready, surrender. Start doing and trust the Universe. You will experience the flow of magic!

Love is essential and it is at the core of everything, but if you miss any one ingredient, it will not work. **Smiling is fundamental: if you lose your smile, you will lose everything.** Life must be joyful, for without joy you cannot experience the divine within you. Remember that you were already born whole and complete. Your body is the ultimate technology; an integrated, intelligent system that sustains your life. Trust this divine intelligence as much as you trust the fact that your next breath will be there for you. If you do not present yourself as an instrument of love on this planet, the experience will not happen as a beautiful dream, but rather as a nightmare.

When I got to know David better, my dear Hanuman, the flying monkey Indian God, he was ready to travel and go on expeditions around Nepal or anywhere at any time. He was ready to fly and take the mountain with him. He could go for days or even weeks, taking only his toothbrush and wings, as that was all he needed. I understood that his soul was light; he was not busy preparing things to carry or preparing to get ready, because he was always ready! He was living with non-attachment and the natural flow of the heart. He was also smiling and laughing all the time. Because of his smiles, everything was easier, even the most difficult moments. And that created the success of our lifetime relationship. Together, we could even cry, and then we would laugh at the cosmic joke and smile back at life!

When I look back, I can clearly see now that choosing love, smiles and trust are *the ingredients* for the manifestation of our dreams. When I go deeper and look at how the past years of my life have manifested dreams with flow—even during challenges and difficult times—the answers that come to me are these three ingredients. My dreams happened only because I was smiling most of the time, between laughter and tears, making decisions based on love and trust. I was ready for whatever challenges came. I believe anyone who uses these ingredients along with gratitude, love and forgiveness will experience the magic of beautiful dreams in life. It is very simple, but most people are not living in such a way. Because they are not truly allowing smiles, love, and compassion into their hearts, they block the experience of living their dreams.

During the 11 years I lived in Nepal, I had the ingredients, but not enough of them. I needed more forgiveness for my ancestors and for humanity as a whole, and I especially needed to learn to be ready, to take action with total surrender and trust. There is no such a thing as half trust. We must trust 100%. There is no doubt that whatever happens is for our highest good. All that happens is exactly what our soul needs to learn at each given moment. Trust it.

And I also had to learn how to laugh louder at the cosmic joke, this big mystery of life, and to smile even more! It was only when we moved to the Philippines and totally let go again that I felt ready to open and blossom, and share love with more and more people. Later, when we moved to Switzerland, I had so many people coming to help and support our project, to create the healing space for the meditation retreats. I felt the flowers had turned into fruits! Life was manifesting my dreams faster and faster, and the rest is history!

What is stopping us from being ready is that we do not know how we can make things happen. We have doubts. We are afraid of just going for it; afraid to jump into the unknown and trust. We overthink things and get frustrated when we don't clearly see the answers; we do not surrender to this divine energy within us and all around us.

Take this very book, for example. I had no idea how I could make it happen, how this old dream would become real. I knew I had to sit down and write, but I could never find enough time, with so many projects going on simultaneously, always multitasking, and with a family to take care of. It was only when I stopped thinking in terms of structures and schedules that it started to happen. I just allowed the creative process to take its course. I was going for morning walks in the forest and started recording myself with my phone. It was a lovely way to work. If I had no time for writing, I would simply walk and speak my truth. And that's how it started. Volunteers later showed up to help me to write it down and correct my grammar.

For me, in every circumstance, the answers of life never come before taking action, they always happen *simultaneously* with the action. They become clear when the movement has already started. Answers arrive when we are already doing something about our circumstances, without much thinking, just stepping forward, with trust—and letting go of expectations. We just do something because we feel it needs to be done. I am not expecting or looking for answers. I just start doing, with trust and surrender to this divine energy, smiling, and with tears of gratitude for this cosmic game!

Although it is essential to dream, we also need to be careful not to get attached to our dreams. Dreams are not desires. They go beyond our ego and limited self. Dreams come from the realms of inspiration and creativity. If you get attached to a dream, it does not fulfil the soul. Not even all the material possessions will be able to fulfil us. The most beautiful dreams happen when we let go and surrender, and put ourselves at the service of this divine intelligence, the consciousness behind it all. With our dreams, we surrender and trust the Universe because this divine intelligence knows what is better for us. Sometimes, with certain intentions, we might be limiting ourselves. The Universe could have given us more than we could imagine, but we limit ourselves by becoming attached to our ideas and expectations.

For example, I dreamed of this 350-year-old house in Switzerland, where I used to live. It was another rainbow story! And if I had made a logical plan for its renovation, it would probably have taken us five years to do what we did in six months. The Universe responded much faster than I could have ever imagined. I was not back in the past, I was not projecting for the future. I was just open and doing what needed to be done, cleaning and cleansing with love, forgiveness, and gratitude. And while I was cleaning and renovating the house, I was taking the opportunity to clean inside of myself. I asked for help from the Universe, but in humbleness I surrendered. So many friends and volunteers showed up, and it was an incredibly amazing journey! I met so many beautiful souls, experiencing such beautiful dreams; and holding a retreat space every summer. It gave me so much hope for humanity! Yes, we are here to rise together, to uplift each other. It brings us such an amazing feeling of gratitude and love when our hearts are open!

Each day we create the conditions to experience this dream. It does not mean getting obsessed with any desire and wanting it to happen. We do what we need to do, but we surrender to this divine intelligence. Whatever happens, happens. No expectations, just TRUST.

It is a great feeling to live in the NOW. To see life flowing beautifully and things happening naturally, as we take action and trust the Universe.

7.
SEEDS OF MUSIC

The power of Sound

Sounds are waves or vibrations that travel through the air and provide human beings with one of the most effective and vital ways of communicating. Sound is a powerful force. It can bring us a sense of peace and well-being. It can also make human beings love, cry, and in some cases be destructive. Everything in existence vibrates, and so we are surrounded by sound all the time.

Sounds affect our nervous system, which controls the body as it receives information from the brain. Some depressing pieces of music can create an earthquake of anxiety in our body and a terrible fight or flight response in us. Music can trigger our brain without us being aware of what it is going on.

One of the most amazing studies on the power of sound was conducted by the japanese scientist Doctor Masaru Emoto, author of the bestselling book *Messages from Water.* Dr. Emoto gained worldwide acclaim for his ground-breaking research and his discovery that water is affected by vibrational sound.

Dr. Emoto analyzed the formation of differently shaped crystals in water as it was exposed to different sounds, such as verbal affirmations, thoughts, music, and even prayers. He focused on verbal affirmations of love and gratitude, and analyzed the water under a microscope, taking pictures before and after to document the changes. Dr. Emoto and his team observed that after the experiment very beautiful crystals had formed where the positive vibrational waves were directed. He then exposed water samples to classical music and found that beautiful crystal shapes formed in these samples as well. He also experimented with people saying things like "you fool," "I will kill you," and other unpleasant phrases using a harsh tone. The findings were that ugly, incomplete, and malformed crystals were formed in the water samples exposed to these negative expressions and tones.

Dr. Emoto concluded that any sound is vibration, and vibrations such as music and other positive sounds, including the human voice, can be a form of healing energy. The vibrations of sounds communicate to one another and produce energy. In nature, vibrations travel via water and air. This is relevant because our human body is approximately 60 percent water and we are definitely very affected by sound.

Sound is a potent, powerful energy that can express love and concern, or cause great pain and destruction. In fact, we live in a magical world where the powerful energy vibrations made by music, positive thoughts, and words of love and harmony produce peace and beauty while vibrations lacking this positive energy produce distortion.

Awakening Through Sound and Music

There is an awakening available if we are able to practice deep listening to nature, and to all music and sounds around us. Music has the power to touch, heal and connect us unlike anything else. From our first moments on Earth, even before we are born, we begin a powerful relationship with sound. The first sound we hear is the soothing rhythm of our mother's heartbeat. Playing or simply listening to music benefits us individually and collectively. The power of music can improve our physical, mental, and emotional health. Music is a source of pleasure and contentment, but it has many other psychological benefits. Music can influence our thoughts, feelings, and behaviours, and has the power to impact our moods and even inspire action. In ancient Greece, music was used in an attempt to cure mental disorders. Even animals and plants can benefit from listening to music.

Music is an integral part of the human experience, from the drumbeats of our ancient ancestors to today's unlimited streaming technology. Healing with sound is believed to date back to ancient times. In 2009, archaeologists excavating a cave in southern Germany uncovered a flute carved from a vulture's wing bone. This delicate artefact is the oldest known musical instrument on Earth—indicating that people have been making music for over 40,000 years.

Music is primordial to all life. And we all can experience its vibration. All life in nature is part of an incredible melodic symphony. Human beings have an amazing power at their disposal and we can learn to use it for healing. Listening to the crickets, to the birds, to the rivers, or the waves can be all we need.

I remember my first silence retreat decades ago at a monastery in Lumbini, the place where Buddha was born, close to the Indian border. It was the end of the monsoon season, and everything around the temple was wet and humid. Hundreds of frogs and crickets would sing simultaneously around the meditation hall, which had glass windows everywhere facing the green. It was warm and all the windows were kept open. During the days, I was so delighted to hear the birds, and during the nights all the sounds were so loud that even if one did speak it would be impossible to hear. I had a mosquito net and a cushion to meditate, and it was amazing to just sit there, nourishing the soul. The sounds of nature were intense, surprisingly healing and delicious. It was exactly what I needed: to be silent and mindful, and to listen to nature. I was deeply grateful for that. It brought me peace and boosted my meditation immensely. Pure nourishment.

If we learn to be silent and listen in such a way, we will discover an entire world that is available to us through sounds and music.

Music's Benefits

Music "selectively activates" our neuro-chemical systems and brain structures associated with positive mood, emotion regulation, attention, and memory in ways that promote immense beneficial changes. It has the power to stabilize emotions, and helps people process their feelings. Music is a powerful way to bring out the best in people.

If you are looking for an easy way to transform your mood, cue the music. Anyone who plays or listens to music knows its effect on their physiological stress response. As listening to calming and relaxing music can help your nervous system recover faster, it improves mood and sleep quality.

The therapeutic effects and mood-boosting benefits of sound and music can evoke emotions, help regain memories, stimulate new neural connections, and improve attention capacity. It can enhance brain functions.

Listening to music in a deep and focused way is a form of meditation, as it tunes our brain waves. The Tibetan monks know this, and use many instruments to this purpose. When I lived in Nepal, I used to visit the Tibetan monasteries often and joined their retreats every year. The incredible power of their instruments can take people into a transcendental experience very quickly. Many instruments are used in Buddhist practices to accompany periods of meditation and chanting. Music therapists, sound healers and yoga practitioners also use gongs, struck and singing bowls, for example, to ease and calm the mind, boost creativity, and expand potential.

Sound can direct the brainwaves in a desired direction. Listening to certain kinds of music and sound can help us to consciously produce and shift our brainwaves.

But while music can uplift us, it can also agitate and unsettle us. Silence can be better than random listening. Putting on the wrong kind of music can actually induce a stress response, leading to stress, mental rumination, and other unhelpful mental states. In this way, music can bolster negative emotions in the same way it can counteract them. Similarly, the sounds of television and films can affect us, even when we are not aware of it.

From a neuroscience point of view, rhythm and other characteristics of the music and sounds we listen to can modulate our heart rates and the activity of our brain's neural networks. Tracks with a slow tempo, gradual chord progression, and drawn-out notes tend to be calming, while chaotic and up-tempo music tends to have the opposite effect. But there's no one piece of music that will do the same thing for everyone. However, the music you choose may say something about your mental health. It is true that music affects the soul, but the effect it has on you depends on the kind of music you listen to.

Music can literally change the brain. Neurological discoveries have proven that music triggers the release of several neurochemicals that play a crucial role in the brain's developmental function and mental health, such as increased dopamine, a chemical associated with pleasure and "reward" centers; decreased stress hormones like cortisol; increased serotonin and other hormones related to immunity; and increased oxytocin, a chemical that fosters the ability to connect to others. It has also shown that music acts as a medium for processing emotions, trauma, and grief; music can also be utilized as a regulating or calming agent for anxiety.

Listed below are some more of the many benefits of listening to music:

- It helps people managing or coping with stress, thus reducing their experience of stress. It also helps people overcome anxiety and depression, encouraging bonding and emotional expression.
- While there are many approaches to treating insomnia, along with other common sleep disorders, listening to relaxing, meditation music can be a safe, effective, and affordable remedy.
- It stimulates the brain and improves our learning capacities. Scientists know that listening to music engages your brain because when looking at MRI scans, they can see the active areas light up in the brain. Furthermore, music has a positive effect on our ability to memorize. Background music can even improve performance in cognitive tasks. Accordingly, playing more upbeat music leads to improvements in processing speed while both upbeat and downbeat music leads to improved memory.
- Music therapy is a safe and effective treatment for a variety of mental disorders, including depression, dementia, stroke, and Parkin-

son's disease. It has no negative side effects, and is therefore a safe and low-risk treatment option.

- It enhances physical performance. Syncing music to our workout allows us to reach peak performance while also using less oxygen. Music acts as a metronome in our body, so it's natural that fast-paced music motivates people to work out harder. It creates more motivation overall. Consider loading up a playlist filled with fast-paced songs that will help boost your motivation and stamina.
- Music has also been proven to reduce pain in operatory procedures. Music is a non-invasive, safe, cheap intervention that should be utilized before undergoing surgery.
- It improves digestion. Playing soft music before or while we eat creates a relaxed setting. We are more likely to eat slowly and, therefore, feel fuller sooner. Many of us often eat with our anxieties and worries, but listening to beautiful music makes us feel calmer, and we're more able to enjoy our meals.
- Music can alter emotional and physiological arousal, much like a sedative. It has the capacity to stimulate people and can aid in recovery. Music helps us sustain healthier lives and even resolve major personal challenges.
- Another important function of music is to create a feeling of cohesion or social connectedness. Music unites and connects us!

Why aren't doctors learning this and teaching it in schools instead of prescribing so many chemicals and medications? Because there is a huge pharmaceutical industry trying to sell drugs at the expense of our health and well-being. But we can become conscious and learn to use music to help heal ourselves. Instead of thinking of music as pure entertainment, consider some of the major mental and physical benefits of incorporating music into your everyday life. You might find that you feel more motivated, relaxed, and happy.

How to Use Music for Mental Health

Music is more than just a form of entertainment, it supports our mental health. But how exactly can we use it in our day-to-day lives?

Focus

Classical and meditation music can help you in maintaining your focus. Music that has a tempo of sixty bpm (beats per minute) increases the efficiency of the brain when processing information. The best way to use it is to have it playing softly in the background as you get on with your tasks. Whenever you are working on a task, consider turning on a little music in the background if you are looking for a boost in your mental performance. Consider choosing instrumental tracks rather than those with complex lyrics, which might end up being more distracting.

Expression

Next time you find it hard to express your emotions, try turning to music for help. You can create your own music, or just listening to music can help you express and process your emotions.

Social connection

Music can stop you from feeling lonely or isolated. Whether it is by playing an instrument, singing, listening, sharing playlists with friends, meditating or dancing with other people, music connects us.

Creativity

Listening to or making music allows your brain to think creatively. So, whether you have a creative project you need to complete or are looking for new ways to improve your mood, try different types of music and see what works best for you.

Relaxation

Music helps you relax. If you choose the right kind of music, change into some comfortable clothes and put your feet up, it's a safe bet that you'll feel relaxed in a matter of seconds. If you need a release and want to feel more energized, just make your body dance, expressing yourself through movement.

Motivation

If you need to clean the house, study, or exercise but you just cannot get off the couch, put on your favorite music to foster some motivation.

Crank up the volume and you will find getting up is much easier than you thought.

What can I do now?

Use music as an aid the next time you feel lonely, or when you need some focus and motivation. Make a playlist of your favorite music, either for yourself or to share with friends. There is plenty of music out there just waiting to be heard.

It is incredible how listening to one song can change everything. It can change the direction of our life's path or even teach us how to live, feel and love. If things are not going right and you do not know what to do, just put on some good uplifting music and clean the house, or maybe just lie down, close your eyes and listen. By incorporating music into your everyday life, you can use it as a tool for good. It has a shifting neurological effect, improves memory, reduces pain, helps to reduce stress, anxiety and depression, and does so much more.

In combination with music, guided meditations are powerful tools; a form of sound healing with voiced instructions. Meditations that involve repeating positive affirmations, chanting or repeating mantras or prayers enhance our strength. It is like a workout for our emotional and spiritual body. Listening to music, playing or singing supports our emotions and invokes the spirit. Music is a powerful ally in taking care of the soil of our inner garden, where the good seeds grow. And best of all, music can make us happy!

The Story of Dalva

Dalva was the wife of my sister's brother-in-law. She was 37 years old and had four children. When she was diagnosed with cancer, the smallest ones, twins, were only two years old and the most beautiful little girls one could imagine. My sister, who is a doctor, was present at Dalva's surgery the day the doctors intended to take the tumor out of her body. Unfortunately, on the operating table, with her abdomen already open, they were shocked to see that the cancer had already spread everywhere. So they decided to close the body and not touch anything because they could not help her anymore. Dalva's life expectancy was no more than six months.

After the surgery, neither her husband nor anyone else had the courage to tell her the truth. He decided that he would do so later at home. But he kept it secret and decided not to say anything, to let her be free of worries for as long as he could. Dalva went home and surprisingly time passed, months were gone and she seemed to be okay, recovered, and feeling well. When she went back to the doctor, to the stupefaction of all, the cancer had disappeared. The doctors were astonished and could not explain what had happened. She was expected to die, but she didn't, and the cancer was gone. Dalva lived for almost another 20 years on this Earth.

I found this story a beautiful healing miracle. When I had the chance to meet Dalva on one of my visits to Brazil, I asked what she did for her healing. She answered she listened to all the happiest songs and music she could, every day. And she would dance while listening to the music. She also told me she had become much more aware of her cells and started having conversations with them while she was going for daily walks. She was sure some people would think she was crazy. Overall, she changed her attitude towards life and her thinking. Her love for her kids and family, together with her boost of happiness, joy and motivation to live healed her. Her cancer disappeared without any chemotherapy or treatment.

This story shows us how the power of music, of happiness, can alter not only our mood but also our physical condition, improve our health and boost our immune system. Dalva used music for healing. Through music we can rewire our energetic system and through consciousness we can reprogram ourselves. Our cells are alive in us. They are intelligent and we can also communicate and speak to them. Believe it or not, your cells can hear you and each of your thoughts and words.

Unfortunately, a decade later, Dalva's cancer reappeared. She would fight for many years, doing chemotherapy and other surgeries, until one day she would eventually die. It was a long journey, but she had seen all her children grow up and they were adults and in university when she left her physical body. It was a victory to go from a life expectancy of a few months to live for almost another 20 years.

What calls my attention in this story is that Dalva did heal herself, but she did not hold on to the changes. As she went back to her old patterns, the cancer returned. She lost the chance to use her experience to share and empower others. I believe when we have the opportunity to cure and heal ourselves, we have the mission to teach others that are suffering in the same way as we were, to help and remind others. And so we keep reminding ourselves too, so we don't forget again what we have learnt.

One night I dreamed of Dalva. In the dream, I asked her to write down her story, as I knew she could help many people. We had not seen each other or spoken for many years, but it was too late. She had died by the time I dreamed of her.

Music Therapy & Intervention

Music can reach places words cannot. Music can be used to enhance and improve lives.

Music therapy and music intervention are holistic approaches to mental healthcare. Music therapy has been used in psychiatric treatments and as prevention measures to help people stay healthy. Music therapists adapt their approach and the music they play to skilfully unlock potential and inspire positive emotions and interactions. They tune in to each movement, reaction, and expression of the person they are working with.

Music therapy benefits a great number of health conditions such as anxiety disorders, depression, post-traumatic stress disorder, dementia, autism, learning difficulties, behavioral and psychiatric disorders and even cancer. Other benefits include decreased stress, blood pressure, and cholesterol levels, reduced risk of coronary artery disease, decreased mood swings and improved sleep.

The term “music interventions” refers to all musical interactions that bring immense benefits to our health, boosting energy and as prevention treatment. Music intervention can be performed by anyone who wishes to use music as medicine for themselves and share with others this knowledge, in order to create a healthy lifestyle.

In other words, music is medicine.

Daniel Levitin, a doctor of neuropsychology, studies the neuroscience of music and how it affects our mental and physical health. Author of the book *This Is Your Brain on Music*, he explains that there is no single “music center” in the brain. Surprisingly, music activates nearly every region of the brain mapped so far.

Levitin was asked if music could replace medicine in some situations. He explained that a lot of things we do affect our physiology just like exercise does. As exercise replaces medicine when it has the desired outcome in terms of our physiology, evidence says that music can alter pain thresholds and increase immune system functions; in addition, it can affect mood and heart and respiration rates. Fast music stimulates the production of adrenaline and other hormones that get your heart racing, thus increasing your pulse and blood pressure, while soothing, relaxing music has the opposite effect.

We are already in a place and time where people are using music as medicine. Many people instinctively choose a certain kind of music for different occasions. If you are having a party, you play one kind of music. If you are relaxing after a long day at the office, you play another type of music. The music you play when you are waking up in the morning is different from the music you play when you are trying to go to sleep at night. A large number of people already use music to suit their desired emotion or mood.

With all the tools and knowledge we now have available we can also cultivate seeds of music for our happiness. We will be able to transform not only ourselves and our surroundings but also contribute to a better quality of life on our planet.

Inner Dance

When I lived in the Philippines, I learned a type of music intervention called inner dance. For two years, I had the opportunity to work and experience a profound, pure, and inspiring lifestyle next to Pi Vilaraza, one of my most beloved teachers. There, I had the opportunity to practice deep listening and letting go. I was on a raw food diet, immersed in daily yoga and healing practices, and got empowered by inner dance, a transformational healing method, rooted in ancient Filipino babaylan (shamanic) tradition. Music then became an instrument of healing.

If I could explain what inner dance is, I would say it is the inner experience that allows you to awaken through music as a language and can take you into the realms of the dreams. It is not dance in physical form, but a dance of insights that happens inside one's soul. As the brain waves shift and produce insights and transformation, they awaken energetic information in the body, which restores and rewires the entire system through sound and vibration.

Inner dance is a transformative shift in consciousness; one that also shifts the physical body. Alongside this shift is the remembrance of our wholeness-oneness, organically leading us to live in harmony with nature. This path leads us to a spiritual life on Earth; an existence of simplicity, sacredness, sustainability. Sound awakening is a movement spreading into many countries, taking many different names and forms. It is powerful force to catapult people into the world of heightened awareness, restoring balance and wholeness.

In the Philippines, I learned that music is a language that can help the soul get into a deep meditative dream state. The person just lies down, closes their eyes, and allows the sounds to enter his/her inner space. The inner dance facilitator helps the person tune in to themselves, directing their attention inwards, and uncovering emotions and feelings that have been locked for a long time. The one who facilitates the music provides a safe space for one to enter this state. In such a state, you can clean and rewire your energetic and nervous system, as you allow the sound to penetrate and enter you fully. You return to yourself by using the power of sound. Music allows us to remember who we truly are.

If you want to enter a meditative dream state yourself, try lying down, closing your eyes and listening to certain kinds of music in deep awareness, along with all the sounds around you. Observe your breath, your heartbeats, and allow the sound to come inside your body, opening yourself up to the experience. Keep doing it and naturally, it will happen. Trust your inner wisdom. You can enter the realm of the dream if you give yourself permission to trust. It is all within you.

Inner dance is an active form of music meditation and intervention. It has helped so many people around the world process their emotions, bringing insights in awakened dreams states, and shifting energy fields. I have witnessed and experienced it.

Some types of sound technology, such as brainwave entrainment or binaural beats, can also be used to stimulate the brain into a specific state. By using pulsing rhythms to align our brainwaves with the frequency of the beat, we can induce enhanced focus and trance states, relaxation, and sleep. Audible brainwave entrainment reduces anxiety, pain, improves behavioural problems and more. Yet, inner dance can go a step further: it takes you on a transcendental journey of dreams; it rewires the energetic system of your body, as it shifts your brain waves, activating awakened dreams states and insights. For many, it brings messages and deep insights of the soul; as the brain automatically adjusts with the frequency of the music you are listening to.

The Process

Inner dance develops intuition by activating the right side of our brain. It is a process of questioning yourself and looking inside. Inner dance uses music as a vehicle to transport you into the dimension of dreams and take you where your soul wants to go.

To begin the inner dance process, we stop everything we are doing and just lie down, tuning ourselves into the frequency of the music and into deep listening. Inner dance is completely subjective, and its success depends on the mental state of the listener. It does not work well if the facilitator is trying too hard to make it happen. It works better when we surrender and trust the process, allowing energy to open up and flow naturally.

The more you trust and surrender, the greater the chance the energetic shift will happen. Simply being in the present moment with an open heart is already an invitation to this force to spontaneously unfold.

Inner dance involves freedom. Though it starts by lying down, it can lead to sitting, moving, dancing, screaming, crying, laughing; everything is allowed, as long as you keep your eyes closed and focus your attention inside yourself, the matrix.

The matrix is the cultural, social, or political environment in which something develops— and includes ourselves. In biology, the matrix is the substance between cells or in which structures are embedded; and in mathematics, it is an organizational structure in which two or more lines of command, responsibility, or communication may run through the same individual. Mix all that with the idea behind the famous science-fiction film *The Matrix*. The whole idea of a virtual world and people living online and in the real world is so much more relevant now than it was in 1999, when the film was produced, and when the internet was still quite nascent. Today, people hide behind social media profiles and virtual reality itself is now a consumer-facing thing. Some people now have virtual reality headsets sat next to the TV that they can put on to enter some crazy world that is completely different to our own. We are much closer now to the world of *The Matrix* than we were in 1999.

During inner dance you might enter another world, a singular world with multiple facets (dimensions, or the matrix). All you need to do is to keep your eyes closed and dive inside yourself.

My inner dance experience reminds me of the film *The Matrix*. In the film, human beings are subjugated by artificial intelligence. The population is placated through the use of a simulated dreamworld, the eponymous "matrix" that bears no small resemblance to our own. That makes it worthy of investigation, as a means of better understanding our own reality.

During inner dance, diverse instruments can be used such as singing bowls, tuning forks, pan flutes, harps, drums, clapping, voice, etc. The facilitator may speak words of encouragement, questioning, singing, moving around or placing their hands on the body of a person to intuitively support the unblocking of energy. Or they may remain still and quiet to let the sounds take effect.

Vibrations can be applied using crystals and stones to release tension and energy, and promote emotional balance for those who are diving inside themselves with courage and trust, surrendering to the process of deep listening.

During the inner dance process, the music activates and shifts certain brainwaves, simulating the sleep cycles produced by our brains. Strictly speaking, our mood is closely linked to the brainwaves we are producing. To alter the brainwaves, the music facilitator plays music that induces relaxation and then accelerates the beats to shift the mood of the person in order to release emotions. There can be two to three rounds of such a process. By the end, the music returns to a more positive and calm state.

Scientists believe intuition operates through the right side of our brain, in the hippocampus and through our gut. Interestingly, the female corpus callosum, the connective white matter that connects our left and right brain hemispheres, is thicker than that of males'. This substantial brain superhighway makes it easier for women to access each hemisphere, further integrating the emotional and gut feelings with the more logical left hemisphere. Women's brains are optimized for rapid intuitive decision making. Women are also more in touch with their emotions, perhaps because they have been given more cultural permission to be this way, and they are more likely to integrate hunches and logic. Because men have a thinner corpus callosum, they are more compartmentalized in their thinking and do not move back and forth from intuition to logic as easily. Although men and women have many physiological differences, of course, we all have the potential to develop intuition; everyone can access this energy.

Inner dance is an experience where we can go beyond our differences and look for balance between our feminine and masculine energies. In the process of accessing, developing, and amplifying our intuition, we must pay attention to our gut. When the neurotransmitters (chemical messengers) in our gut fire up, we might feel "butterflies" or a queasy sensation. It is not by accident that we use the terms "intuition" and "gut feeling" interchangeably. Science has already shown us that our gut has a brain of its own—a second brain so to speak. In fact, our gut has an entire network of neurotransmitters called the enteric nervous system.

During the inner dance process, a lot is happening energetically, specifically in the solar plexus, mostly because many of us need cleansing to unblock the area in order to activate and open up the energetic flow to the heart and higher chakras, our energy centers. Later in the book we will have an entire section on the chakras in our bodies.

The more we dive inside ourselves, the more we find out that we already have everything we are searching for. We just need to trust and listen quietly, and all the answers can be found. This happens when we pause and are present, engaged in deep listening and breathing.

Pay attention to your energy. What is your intuition telling you? What is your gut feeling? How do you feel? Drained or energized? Are you taking care of your seeds? Quiet your mind and reflect upon these questions for a moment.

Inner dance works by letting go, trusting and surrendering, just as every other spiritual path does. Everything is a part of the whole, of this cosmic game. Trust that there is a supreme intelligence holding life together and creating a space for us to live and experience a human life. Trust that the Universe is providing you with what you need at each moment, and what you need for growth whilst understanding where you are coming from and where you want to go. The Universe mirrors you, your mind, your consciousness. Inner dance welcomes you to the realm of dreams.

In the human brain anything we imagine or visualize internally feels exactly the same as if we were experiencing it in reality. Scientific studies have proven that the brain makes no difference between visualization and reality. This is one way in which we create and transform our realities along with our consciousness. Inner dance is a wonderful tool for that.

My dreams have become memories stored inside my body. Dreams can be a portal, a doorway to many awakenings. We can dive into awakened dream states without going to sleep. Music can take us there with its vibrational frequencies if we let go and surrender to the sound without any expectations.

There are no rules; for some it might present itself in one way, for others in a very different way. It can present itself in so many variations because in fact, it is like water. It can take many forms. We cannot hold it. It is spirit, energy, and it is free. This energy exists and is very powerful, even though it cannot be seen.

During the inner dance process, whatever comes to the surface is inside our being and somehow inside the collective consciousness too. We can only embrace, look at it, accept, reflect upon, and sit with it. This is a process of cleansing, growth, and awakening through music. We have polluted our oceans and rivers, and so many of us have polluted our bodies and minds too. There is a lot to clean inside ourselves. We also carry memories of suffering from our ancestors and humanity. So many of us have a lot of cleansing to do in our energetic system, and we can do so by using sounds. Sound can break a window, sound can open us.

All this inner work may intimidate people, but it is all okay. We are a work in progress, and with compassion and good seeds we will heal everything that needs to be healed. As we start to clean ourselves, we start to shine from the inside out, from the depths of the soul.

This process can make you cry, laugh, scream, yell, whatever; it is powerful. You will feel the joy of being who you truly are, and you will feel how an expansion of consciousness creates stronger bonds between you and the people around you. You will finally give yourself the opportunity to be in the here and now. I call this freedom, I call this love.

Ecstatic Dance

In its pure state, music takes us into trance without the need of any other substance. Music is a very complex, multi-dimensional set of stimuli. It involves rhythm, timbre, pitch, and volume, and it is always fluctuating. Music is a way to bypass our rational side and get in touch with the emotional side that is often hidden.

On one of my visits to Thailand while I lived in Switzerland, I got in touch with the ecstatic dance movement on Ko Phan Ghan island.

Ecstatic dance evolved from the conscious dance movement meditations, yoga, and somatic therapies on the west coast of the US and Hawaii. It flowered as a free-form dance playground in which the music is the leader and participants are free to weave their way through the different soundscapes. The dancers abandon themselves to the rhythm and move freely as the music takes them, leading to trance and a feeling of ecstasy.

It is a sacred free-form playground for the embodiment of Spirit where dance blossoms, Spirit awakens, boundaries melt, boredom dissolves, creativity breaks out, playfulness comes alive, hope emerges, prayers are heard, beauty flows, communities collaborate, ritual is reinvented and harmony resonates as the beat deepens within an electronic tapestry of world rhythms, weaving us together as one great family.

From the description above one can tell how much I love it! With my previous experience of inner dance, ecstatic dance seemed to be another form with similar content; another way of presenting an awakening through music. For me, ecstatic dance and inner dance both come from the same source and have the same principle: that sound and music can help us to heal.

Through music and movement you can experience the freedom and joy of your soul, and you can use it to uncover and open up new dimensions of yourself, on the way to liberation. Music and dancing are primordial to living beings of all times.

The facilitator of ecstatic dance is the holistic DJ who plays the music throughout the session. During the ecstatic dance, all ranges of brainwaves will be experienced, similar to inner dance. Ecstatic dance is a free-form, unstructured dance space, driven by carefully crafted music with the intention of creating a healing journey. No dance experience or partner is necessary. During the ecstatic dance session, the eyes can be closed as it is an inner experience. Closing the eyes helps you explore the energetic field around your body, in slow and fast motion and as you allow the beats to take you into the journey.

The music and sounds guide people to dance and will support them on this journey of joy and liberation. The body is expressing itself, and as you free your movement, your soul is directly affected.

The effect of ecstatic dance is ecstasy itself, which may be experienced to differing degrees. Dancers are described as feeling connected to others, and to their own emotions. The dance serves as a form of meditation, helping people to cope with stress and attain serenity. A form of awakening through sound and movement, it also uses a large range of rhythms and produces a shift of brainwaves.

Ecstatic dance is an environment without observers, judgments, posturing, attitudes, conversations, shoes, alcohol, fragrances or smoke. It is a space where everyone can feel safe. This is the dance you dance when nobody is watching; allowing your body to move freely without judgments or concerns for the grace or beauty of the dance, just getting lost in the dance in a space of no-mind.

Ecstatic dance empowers people of all shapes, ages, sizes and backgrounds to freely express themselves. The liberating atmosphere creates a melting pot of acceptance, and the fearlessness with which others move gives everyone permission and courage to dance without inhibition. Everyone is welcome!

Ultimately, ecstatic dance is a spiritual practice. It creates a safe space to explore healing through communion, individually and with your community/tribe, with the divine through dancing, without the interactions of the mind while talking and drinking, common in the nightclub scene. During ecstatic dance you have no one to impress—our attention is focused on yourself not on others—so you can be utterly yourself, getting down, letting loose, allowing your emotions, dreams and prayers to dance themselves, freeing your mind and body in a safe and healthy way.

Ecstatic dance is an inner/outer journey, an authentic moving meditation where true presence is experienced. It creates a direct body-mind-spirit connection, allowing our body and inner guide to be our teacher. It's about being fully present, using this movement and energetic experience to release stuck patterns in our bodies, emotions and mind and being able to experience blessings and union with the divine.

The inner dance and ecstatic dance communities showed me one of the best approaches to life I had found so far. I had found my tribe!

PART II:
SCIENCE & PRACTICE

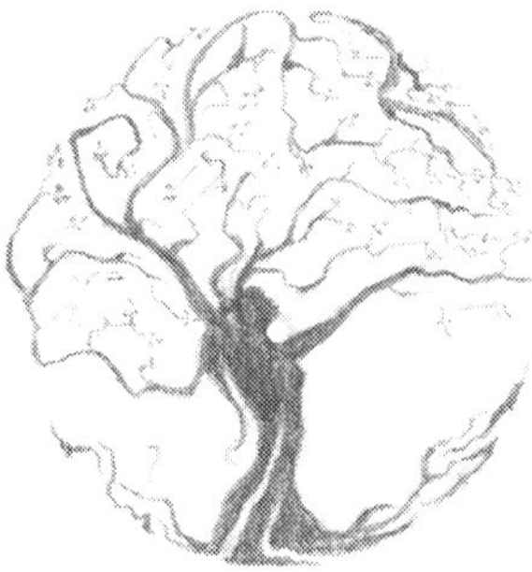

"All religions, arts and sciences are branches of the same tree."
Albert Einstein

8.
THE MIND AND THOUGHTS

BRAINWAVES

We are surrounded by energy in the form of waves, sounds, and vibrations. This includes frequency waves from satellites, radio/television and wireless internet, but also sound vibrations from the wind rushing through the feathers of a hawk or the leaves of a tree. Our brains also have frequencies.

The brain is an electrochemical organ which oscillates at different frequencies along a spectrum reflecting regions and networks that correspond to particular processes, thoughts, and sensations.

At the root of all our thoughts, emotions, and behaviours lies the communication between neurons within our brain. Brainwaves are produced by synchronized electrical pulses from masses of neurons communicating with each other. It's a vibratory frequency. When many neurons interact at the same time, this activity is strong enough to be detected even outside.

Brainwaves were scientifically detected by placing electrodes on the scalp. This activity is then amplified, analyzed, and visualized. This is electroencephalography, or EEG—a fancy word that just means electrical brain graph. Scientists found that we have a kind of a continuous spectrum of consciousness, from slow, to loud and functional, to fast, subtle, and complex.

We could also think of brainwaves as musical notes, or like a symphony. The higher and lower frequencies link and connect to each other through harmonics. Our brainwaves change according to our feelings and actions. With some brainwaves, we can feel tired, slow, sluggish, or dreamy, and with others, we feel wired, energized and hyper-alert.

These waves range in various cycles per second (CPS), or hertz, and are called Gamma, Beta, Alpha, Theta, and Delta. The classification of brainwave states remains constant across all human beings. One way that brainwaves convey information via EEG is through their rate of repetition. Some oscillations occur at more than thirty cycles per second (and up to 100 cycles per second). These cycles, also called frequencies, are measured in hertz (Hz). As we'll see, these different brainwaves correspond to different states of thought or experience.

What do brainwaves mean to us? Why are they important? When our brainwaves are out of balance, there can be corresponding problems in our emotional and neuro-physical health. Research has identified brainwave patterns associated with all sorts of emotional and neurological conditions, linking them to anxiety disorders, sleep problems, hyper-vigilance, impulsive behaviour, anger/aggression, agitated depression, chronic nerve pain and spasticity, and ADHD.

We feel tension or stress when we produce Beta brainwaves, and we feel relaxed and creative when we produce Alpha brainwaves. We transform feelings into action when we generate Theta brainwaves, and we feel deep insight and wisdom when we generate Delta brainwaves.

Instabilities in brain rhythms are proven to correlate with neurological and mental disorders, such as bruxism, panic attacks, bipolar disorder, migraines, narcolepsy, epilepsy, sleep apnea, vertigo, tinnitus, eating disorders, diabetes, hypoglycemia and aggressive behaviour. Our brains are always producing waves, and they certainly correlate with the very basics of our mental, physical and spiritual health.

On the opposite side, brainwave training through traditional eastern methods such as meditation and yoga can bring your brainwaves into balance in a natural way. All in all, depending on the frequencies being tuned into, your perception of reality shifts. Your brains is like a radio: you tune it and you get to that frequency. Any process that changes your perception will change your brainwaves. Chemical interventions such as medications and recreational drugs are the most common artificial way to alter brain function.

FIVE TYPES OF BRAINWAVES

The different patterns of brainwaves can be recognized by their amplitudes and frequencies. They can then be categorized based on their level of activity or frequency, related to our experience of being, thinking, and perceiving.

- **Slow activity** refers to a low frequency (the rate of waves) and high amplitude (the distance between two peaks of a wave). These oscillations are often much larger in amplitude (wave depth). For example: the low and deep beat of a drum.
- **Fast activity** refers to a higher frequency and often smaller amplitude. For example: high-pitched flute, or a high-pitched voice.

GAMMA BRAINWAVES

- Frequency: 32 – 100 Hz
- Associated state: Heightened perception, learning, problem-solving tasks

Gamma brainwaves are the fastest measurable EEG brainwaves and have been equated to a "heightened perception", or "peak mental state" in which there is a simultaneous processing of information from different parts of the brain. Gamma brainwaves are shown to be much stronger and more regularly observed in very long-term meditators such as Buddhist monks.

Gamma brainwaves pass information rapidly and quietly. The most subtle of the brainwave frequencies, the mind has to be quiet to access Gamma. Gamma was dismissed as "spare brain noise" until researchers discovered it was highly active in states of universal love, altruism, and the higher virtues. Gamma is also above the frequency of neuronal firing, which is the normal process of communication between neurons through electrical impulses and neurotransmitters, so how it is generated remains a mystery. It is speculated that Gamma rhythms also modulate perception and consciousness, and that increased presence of gamma waves corresponds to expanded consciousness and spiritual awakening.

BETA BRAINWAVES

- Frequency:13-32 Hz
- Associated State: Alert, active thinking, tension, stress

Beta brainwaves are easiest to detect when we're busy and actively thinking. Beta brainwaves dominate the normal waking state of consciousness for most people when attention is directed towards cognitive tasks and the outside world. Beta is a fast activity, present when we are engaged in:

- Active conversation
- Decision making
- Problem solving
- Focusing on a task
- Learning a new concept

They are also very dense and will produce cortisol in the body, a stress hormone which, with time, can create energetic blockages in our system.

ALPHA BRAINWAVES

- Frequency: 8-12 Hz
- State: Physically and mentally relaxed

Alpha waves occurs at different stages of the wake-sleep cycle. It is more frequent during the relaxed mental state; predominantly during wakeful relaxation with closed eyes. Alpha frequency is a state of relaxation that induces creativity.

Occurrence of alpha wave activity also happens during REM sleep, but the reason is not yet fully understood by science.

- The process of falling asleep
- Being creative and artistic

When we produce Alpha brainwaves, we allow the energy to flow more freely and we are more at ease with life. Alpha brainwaves are dominant during quietly flowing thoughts and in some meditative states. Alpha is a resting state for the brain, focused in the now and experiencing the present moment. Overall, Alpha waves aid mental coordination, calmness, alertness, mind/body integration and learning. When you listen to soft, relaxing music, your brain starts to get into the same frequency.

THETA BRAINWAVES

- Frequency: 4-8 Hz
- State: Creativity, insight, dreams, reduced consciousness

According to Professor Jim Lagopoulos of Sydney University, “Previous studies have shown that Theta waves indicate deep relaxation and occur more frequently in highly experienced meditation practitioners. The source is probably frontal parts of the brain, which are associated with monitoring other mental processes.”

Theta brainwaves are most frequently detectable in the dream state, but they can also be seen during:

- Deep meditation
- Daydreaming

Research has also shown a positive association of Theta waves with memory, creativity and psychological well-being. Theta is our gateway to learning, memory, and intuition. In Theta, our senses are withdrawn from the external world and focused on signals originating from within. It's also where we hold our "stuff": our fears, troubled history, and nightmares.

DELTA BRAINWAVES

- Frequency: 0.5-4 Hz
- State: Deep sleep

These are the slowest of all brainwaves and are strongest when we are enjoying restorative sleep in a dreamless state. This is also the state where healing and rejuvenation are stimulated. Delta brainwaves have a loud and low frequency, and they're deeply penetrating, like a drumbeat. Delta waves suspend external awareness and are the source of empathy. [1]

---

1 Lagopoulos et al. "Increased Theta and Alpha EEG Activity During Nondirective Meditation." *The Journal of Alternative and Complementary Medicine*, 2009; 15 (11): 1187 DOI: 10.1089/acm.2009.0113

Is it possible to change how much we experience these different brainwaves, brain states, and thought experiences associated with them? Neuroscience has proven it is possible to consciously change our brainwaves. As research indicates, there are significant differences between the brainwaves of highly experienced meditators and common people. Expert meditators not only have different resting-state brainwaves from non-meditators, but they also seem able to control their brainwaves with greater ease.

What is interesting is how we can become more aware of which kinds of brainwaves we are producing and how we can benefit from them. I, myself, with practice have been able to detect and feel which brainwave I am producing at a certain moment. At the same time, I have become more aware and sensitive to the brainwaves of the people around me, by simply sensing their presence and energy.

We feel tension or stress when we produce Beta brainwaves, and we feel relaxed and creative when we produce Alpha brainwaves. We transform feelings into action when we generate Theta brain waves, and we feel deep insight and wisdom when we generate Delta brainwaves.

These brainwave-changing skills can be learned through meditating. Meditation deepens our ability to focus on and control our attention. We will go through it together. The meditation techniques you will learn in this book are very simple and you will be able to experience and feel the changes in your brainwaves. Your energy will naturally increase, and with a little practice you will be able to feel the shift.

Thoughts Are Creative Energy

Through our thoughts, we can manifest the life and the dreams we want. We can also use our thoughts to access different levels of information as if we were entering a cosmic library. The left side of our brain is mainly the logical and intellectual operational system, while the right side is related to our feelings and intuition. We want to activate both sides of our brain to connect mind and thoughts to feelings and heart. When they are both activated, the pituitary gland, located in our third eye, is also activated, and we experience wisdom and the wholeness of who we truly are.

Our brain has the capacity to process vast amounts of information within a millisecond, yet there is still a lot we do not know about the brain's functions. Science usually separates the mind and heart, utilizing more the logical, left side of the brain. It wasn't until recently that science started to connect the two.

Through meditation or simple observation, we can learn to guide our thoughts and master our emotions. Our thinking is not who we are, it is merely a set of codes, just as software is to a computer. With practice and awareness, we develop our ability to recognize and change our software programs. If the previous program was bugging or did not help you to be happy, make the necessary changes to reprogram yourself and as you do so you will see the results.

When I talk about programs, I also refer to how feelings affect our words, and vice versa. Words are the way a program is translated. Words alone have no intrinsic meaning. What gives value to words are the programs from which they originate. If you, like a baby, do not speak any language at all, there will not be any specific meaning attached to the words you hear, but feelings occur as sounds are being pronounced or heard. On the contrary, if you do speak a certain language and I tell you a specific word, you might then experience memories or feelings that are related to that word, such as fear or joy.

Not long ago, a lady told me that she was afraid of using mantras because, for her, certain words can have too much power. I told her that we are the ones who empower words with our programming, not the other way around. If someone's brain is damaged, that person will not be able to use his/her brain to run a program, making this person unable to interpret or give meaning to words. Indeed, we are the ones who process the words and give meaning to them. In this lady's case, because of her programming, the feelings associated with the word "mantra" were bringing her fear, but that was only because of her prior learned beliefs.

Fear is a bugged program, a malware that is interfering and limiting our potential as human beings. In the prehistoric era, fear arose as an instinctive survival program, from the times when our ancestors had to run away from danger. But in today's modern world, fear is misused, mainly as a means of control. Truly, it is possible to overcome fear by changing our mental programs. It is all about how we see it, how we teach and guide our own minds, and how we deal with our emotions while at the same time being conscious of them.

Fear and anger are destructive mental programs. We can observe and embrace with compassion any negative thoughts or emotions that come to our mind and body. Be aware of its poison but in evolutionary terms, we know that all emotions were part of our survival kit. In psychological terms these emotions are guidepost to examine and to understand their source and then deal with their cause. Pushing away so-called negative emotions only makes them retreat deeper inside us and cause secret wounding. As we observe, accept and heal what arises, we can examine it with a compassionate presence and kindness. All emotions can teach us something about ourselves. We can, from now on, make choices of emotions and thoughts we want to run in everyday life and in our system.

Some of the programs I mainly use are trust and surrender, it brings me so many positive benefits and outcomes. But beware not to identify yourself with any certain program. Deep down, you are not the program you are running. You are an incredible divine being that has the power to run anything you want in your system. When we understand this, we just select and create our programs consciously. Next, we take control and guide our own mind, our operational system.

All these mental programs we run have consequences, just like the fruits that grow inside us, depending on the type of seeds we are watering, so the programs we run depend on our own choices. Choose the seeds you want to plant in the garden as well as the programs you want to run in your software. Choose seeds and programs of gratitude, of compassion, of love, of peace... They are wonderful.

It is important to acknowledge that the repetitive patterns of our minds are just programs that can either elevate or devalue us. I have installed a couple of cleaning programs that help me remove the garbage of past memories from my subconscious mind. The main way I do this is by being grateful for everything. I express my gratitude as frequently as possible, repeating to myself, "Thank you, thank you, thank you..." as a mantra. Also, I send all my love into the Universe and to Mother Earth by telling this divine energy, "I love you, I love you, I love you..." These are two affirmations or mantras I have been saying for many years now, and they have worked wonders for me. In a later chapter, I will be sharing all of these practices with you.

Hardware and Software

Like heads and tails, inner gardening and mental reprogramming are just different sides of the same coin. In other words, while inner gardening is like the poet, connected to the right side of our brain, mental reprogramming is like the engineer, closely related to the left side of our brain. The different perspectives work together to express consciousness.

We have a sophisticated inner technology, an advanced and intelligent engineering structure manifesting in this intricate matrix within our bodies. In short, the hardware is our body and the software is our thoughts. How it works and how we use it determines how we exist in this life.

The quality of the software, and the drivers we install in our systems, depends on our vibration and frequency, on what we think and how we act. We can all tune in to the vibration and frequency of love and beauty that is, at every moment, around and within us. Gratitude, love, and forgiveness are amazing programs and some of the best drivers one can have for happiness. They contain everything we need to operate our system effectively to connect with the Universe.

We have choices, courage, and an amazing planet on which to enjoy this beautiful life. We have Mother Earth giving us everything we need. We do not need to be afraid to fall into the unknown, to surrender and loosen our grip. The more we let go, the more we open up to this energy and let it come through us.

We are the creators of our reality, and so we must take 100% responsibility for all our choices. If you think others are making choices for you, it is because you are allowing that to happen. If you are distracting yourself all the time, that is also your choice. The way you are living your life is and always will be your choice.

So many people have channeled and received this same information, which comes not only in the form of language, but also in the form of experience. The more you channel it, the more you tune your heart into the love frequency, and the more you experience life in a blissful state. From there, you deepen the connection with your heart, creating coherence between your thoughts, words, and actions. We can choose to be either connected or disconnected to these programs. Actually, most people are just connected to the internet and are totally disconnected from nature, from their hearts and from the present moment.

> *By tuning into gratitude, we have the key that opens all the doors. We can shift and we can enter a new level of consciousness.*

All of our experiences and belief systems are like programs that we run according to our upbringing and society. They are like software installed on the computer of our mind and stored in our memory: memories from this life, past lives, and even from our ancestors. The mind is full of thoughts, and consequently, full of problems too. We create these problems, and if we look deeply, they really only exist in our mind. In the same way, it is also possible to see beauty everywhere; the difference lies in the mental programs we are running.

Thus, if we see problems everywhere, we will think the world is a miserable place. But if we see beauty everywhere, we will regard the world as wonderful. It is up to us to see and change the programs installed in us by training our mind and opening our eyes. If we want to see beauty, we can find beauty.

What do you want to see and experience? Think about it and it will become true for you. If you feel you are not good enough, understand that it is just your mental programming; it is not the truth. You are an amazing human being with infinite potential—this is your truth! Everything else is just a conditioning factor that rambles around your mind; that relates to your upbringing, cultural and social values, etc. Conditioning is a response to a stimulus in the environment, such as rewards and punishments, or your own behaviors regarding significant events, that stem from your experiences since birth. Your conditionings affects your thoughts and emotions, and becomes something you accept as truth; it creates your perceptions of the truth. These perceptions can be either accurate or inaccurate, and every time you have a false perception, suffering occurs. In most cases, your perceptions are inaccurate, and you suffer because you are too sure of them.

Many of us are running programs with thoughts and ideas that do not help us to be happy in our lives. What we focus on becomes true: this is how we install programs in our minds. Hence, if we do not change the programs, we cannot change our experiences. We need to understand that our thoughts (our programs) are creating our experiences. Nothing is really happening outside ourselves. What manifests in the physical world starts inside us, in our own energy field.

What would happen, then, if you changed and created your own programs? I have met a lot of people who took the opportunity to learn from their suffering to become more loving and compassionate people. Their pain and betrayals became their greatest teachers. They understand that most people who hurt others are like blind people—they cannot see, and they act out of ignorance. Compassionate people have learned to forgive.

We can still take care of ourselves and our own lives by learning to be better people. All in all, our thoughts and beliefs are just like programs, and by understanding how they work we can learn how to uninstall those that we do not want or that no longer serve us. Let us install programs based on love, compassion and gratitude so we can create a beautiful reality for our lives.

Rebooting the System with Meditation

There are many forms of meditation that can make our lives better. Not all meditation forms require you to sit and be still. Sitting is one form of meditation, maybe a good one to begin with, as you create a healthy habit of calming the mind in a direct way. Indeed, other forms of meditation, such as inner dance and mindfulness, might bring us to the awareness of the present moment in a more engaged and active way.

In my opinion, the most important part of meditation is not even the technique, but the heart, the feelings, the thoughts, and the awareness we have while doing whatever we are doing. It is not the time spent sitting, but the love that we feel and cultivate in our daily lives, and the service we do to our planet and to humanity. It does not matter if we are sitting quietly, walking, washing the dishes or cleaning the floor, so long as we keep smiling and sharing our love with others and with life. In the end, it is all about love, gratitude, and forgiveness.

Meditation allows us to move from Alpha to Delta brainwaves consciously, without having to go into a sleep state. With it comes the positive effect of recharging ourselves in all aspects: physically, mentally, and spiritually. For some, one hour of deep meditation is equivalent to three hours of sleep. If we start meditating and living in such a way, we will increase vibrant energy in us and our surroundings. Afterwards, meditation expands to everything in life. It is not about sitting anymore—that was maybe the beginning. It becomes then an engaged meditation in its advanced form, in everything we do. It is about being aware, mindful of everything, and in love with life. Remember, nothing is separate. Our meditation becomes an integrated part of our lives, all the time.

When we are producing a lot of Beta brainwaves, we often find ourselves in a highly sensitive, irritated, and stressed mood. This is when our cortisol levels spike and make us way more reactionary, and sometimes irrational. If we obtain the ability to recognize what brainwave state we are in, and the characteristics of each one, simply by observing our emotions, we will be able to approach situations with more compassion for ourselves and for others. It starts with a practice of observation. You may find that regular meditators are often a lot more mindful, calm, and creative. These lasting effects happen because meditators are skilled at observing their thoughts. We become aware when any toxic or negative ideas emerge, taking care of cleansing our system from inside.

Ironically, when our brains are performing at an intense and continuous rate, we are more prone to act counterproductively, even listlessly. It is so easy to lose control of our thoughts and actions, and that is why meditation is so important; and for us to have the ability and the freedom to consciously shift our brainwaves. We have all had those dreaded days where it's hard to wake up, and everything is chaotic and cluttered. More often than not, by the time we get around to the task at hand, our brains feel completely frazzled, and we're seething with anxiety, and start projecting our anger onto others.

Too many of us are burnt out. Those dense Beta waves and raised cortisol levels are as useless as garbage is for unclogging your drain. But if you take a moment to pause, breathe in and out slowly, go for a mindful walk or sit down and cool off, you can regain equilibrium. This break is essential for the brain to enter the Alpha state, to slow down and go into deeper states of consciousness, bringing us back to a more loving and productive headspace.

Meditation opens many doors by which we can become the true administrator of ourselves, our own operating system. This, in turn, provides us with the ability to debug unconscious programs and background processes that may be disrupting and hindering our daily functions. When we realize that most of our problems come from the software we are running, we can truly reboot ourselves. The hardware, our body, is simply amazing. The problem is in the software that is running it, how the mind operates. Therefore, it is vital that we install new programs in ourselves. We have the capacity to reboot the system whenever we choose. We can start by taking the simple steps of closing our eyes, watching our breath, letting our thoughts pass over like clouds in the sky, and just relaxing and observing it. Filling up ourselves with love, forgiveness, and gratitude.

I remember when I first started practicing meditation. I felt like my brain was crazy, and I could not focus on my breath or on a simple mantra without the disturbance of so many thoughts coming and going, like turbulent waves in the sea. It was frustrating at the beginning, a wild horse, but with determination and some mental training, my mind softened and calmed down. My mind then became my best friend.

From that moment on, I learned to help myself and raise the energy flow inside my body. I could then observe how the energy flow in most people's bodies was so blocked, and that was why so many people were physically, mentally, and spiritually sick. Later, I came to understand that because I had opened my own heart and freed myself, my mission in life was to help others to open their hearts, allow their energy to flow, and free themselves too. It was the gift of life! I learned to trust my feelings and heart, deciding to accept myself even if I sounded strange or crazy to many people.

As time goes by, meditation becomes easier. Even for a well-trained mind, it is always a continuous process of observation and inner work. Just as you clean and feed your body every day, you clean and feed your mind and spirit too. You take care of your body, mind, and your spirit. If you do not do that, with time, you can get sick. Sadly, mental disorders, such as depression, are very common in today's world. Prevention is the best way to keep ourselves healthy. We do not need to become sick to ask for help; rather we can take care of ourselves now before it is too late.

Some techniques such breath awareness and mantras, meaningful words repeated internally with great feeling, can ease the mind. You become the observer. You understand that you have the power to guide your mind in whichever direction you choose. And your mind will help you. With time, we tune this mind state into our waking lives and develop our true compassionate and loving nature, even in high-stress areas. Rather than panicking, running around trying to gather our things and get everything ready, we take a minute to slow down our brain and get it into the "Alpha gear." It might be exactly what you need to get through "those days" with a smile on your face.

Let us tune into this frequency to heal ourselves and subsequently make the world a brighter, more heavenly place! Let us connect not only through the frequencies of digital devices but rather through the all-encompassing frequency of love, through our hearts and minds. Let us hold hands not only as individuals but as one universal family full of joy, fulfilment, peace, and love.

Meditation and the Mind

I once heard somebody say that meditation was about shutting down the mind. This person spoke as if our thoughts were our enemies. As if we had to fight them and be careful of their perils. For some people, it can seem that way, but there are other ways of seeing and experiencing thoughts. Conversely, you can make peace with your mind, turning your thoughts into your friends by guiding them in a loving direction. If you train your mind in that way, it will then work for you, not against you, having tremendous power and a positive impact on your life.

Meditation is a very general term and there are a lot of misleading notions around it. However, to put it simply, meditation is about cultivating and becoming familiar with the way the mind works. We understand that meditation is a path that leads to happiness, and that there are many types of meditation available for us to learn and practice.

Meditation is strictly related to neuroplasticity. This term refers to the process of loosening the old nerve cells to make space for new ones to emerge. In other words, neuroplasticity is the brain's ability to adapt, form new connections and pathways, and change how its circuits are wired. Neurogenesis, on the other hand, is the brain's ability to grow new neurons. Proponents of mindfulness meditation have long believed meditation can cause physical changes in the brain; as it turns out, they were right! Many studies have shown that meditation can help people who suffer from severe depression and reduce the risk of relapse by up to 40 percent. Mindfulness meditation can, in fact, improve brain function.

Our brains are truly extraordinary. Unlike computers, which are built to certain specifications and can only update their software, our brains can actually update both their software and hardware. When we learn something new, we create new connections between our neurons. We rewire our brains to adapt to new circumstances. This happens daily and automatically, but it's also something we can consciously direct. Our minds have the incredible capacity to both alter the strength of connections among neurons, essentially rewiring them, and to create entirely new pathways.

The brain is effectively rewired through meditation; as your feelings and thoughts deepen in your heart, your brain is actually transforming both mentally and physically. In fact, several areas of the brain become larger after meditation, such as the hippocampus and the fight-or-flight response system in the amygdala.

The more mindful we become and the more we meditate, the more it becomes our default state. This is why mindfulness meditation has such a big impact on regular practitioners; they have taught their brain to be calm, peaceful, and centered all throughout the day, not just during sitting meditation. Through meditation, you can reframe your whole world and rewire your brain so that you are more objective. You have the power to see things as they are, and you can respond thoughtfully, deliberately, and effectively to everything you experience. The science behind meditation's effect on the brain is enough to invite you to take a few cleansing breaths before continuing with this book!

> *"Any man could, if he were so inclined, be the sculptor of his own brain."*
> *Santiago Ramón y Cajal*

To meditate is to tune in to the heart, to develop awareness, mindfulness, concentration, and insight. Through meditation we learn to observe our thoughts and feelings, and we can shift the realities and frequencies we experience in our lives.

Through this practice, we learn how energy works and experience it within ourselves. All techniques presented in the following chapters have the same intention: to share tools to improve the quality of our lives. And to help you find practical methods to support your journey.

I hope somehow it will inspire others and that we all become better people every day, always growing, evolving, learning, no matter how old we are. For me, life is about sharing. Meditation itself is just a tool that helps to tune ourselves and activate our hearts. It can take many forms, but most of all, it is an awakening to the magic of life, to cultivating good seeds, trusting and surrendering to this divine intelligence without fear. Somehow this is my mission, to share such experiences and to inspire others to live out of love. We can experience heaven on Earth! Heaven is not for when we die. We have all the conditions we need.

After understanding about brainwaves and the energy frequencies we are creating by our thinking mode, we can become more conscious of them.

In the next section, you will find a simple explanation about the chakras and related practices.

9.
CHAKRAS

PSYCHOLOGY, ENERGY, AND CHAKRAS

My psychology thesis was titled "The Ego as a Social Illusion." I wrote about how I believed that everything said in traditional psychology is true on one level, but that human existence was far beyond all of it. When I wrote my thesis, I was inspired by Ken Wilber, an incredible writer on transpersonal psychology and integral theory. Wilber explains that everything everyone says is correct, even if it does not seem so. It is just that people are speaking on different levels of consciousness. We are all speaking from different realities, similar to looking at the same object through the lens of different sunglasses, and different colors. All that is said is true from the different realities in which we exist.

Chakras are the energy centers of our body. In Yoga philosophy, it is known that we have seven energy centers where the chakras reside, and each one vibrates at a different frequency and with different emotions. They are the core elements of an energetic system that communicates with the body via biological networks, such as the endocrine glands and nervous system, to keep it balanced and healthy.

The different levels of consciousness we live in are related to the energetic system operating in each chakra. This determines how each chakra is activated, flowing or blocked energetically in our bodies.

The Sanskrit word "chakra" translates to "wheel" or "disc." Think of the chakras as spinning wheels of energy located at different spots along your spine. There are seven chakras that begin at the base of your spine and move upward, ending with the seventh on the crown of your head. Each chakra has an energetic realm that it rules. When energy cannot flow freely between the chakras, we become physically or mentally ill.

Before most sickness presents itself in its physical form, it happens first on an energetic level. Life contains suffering, but despite this, when the energy flows up into our hearts and through our bodies, we experience pure joy and happiness. All negative emotions, such as anger, grief, and sadness can lead us to depression or other mental or physical illnesses. But this happens only when the energy in our lower chakras is blocked and not flowing up to the heart and other energy centers.

Meditation is a way by which we can literally pump up this energy, to make it flow upwards, opening and unblocking the energy centers and allowing the energy to circulate freely. Meditation, visualization, affirmations, mantras and pure heart intention make a powerful combination that opens the energetic systems in our bodies.

Freud's theories had great influence on our civilization's psychology framework. His theories explaining personality development, and the psychoanalytic and sexual theories, would seem to describe the lower chakras quite well. But they completely ignored the dimensions of the higher chakras. Most of what I learned in years of psychology studies at university seemed so limited. As students, we were forced to learn all of that and ignore the most beautiful and amazing aspects of human life. It was quite a surprise for me to discover that the psychology theories were so limited. I guess it might be the same with medicine, where students need to learn to treat sickness using drugs, instead of promoting true health and happiness. It prevents us from seeing our wholeness.

In terms of raising the energy to the upper chakras, when the energy goes up to the heart, it is another story. It is all about love, compassion, forgiveness and the most beautiful aspects of human beings. The philosophy of the chakras is very complete. It does not deny the lower chakras, but integrates all of them in multiple dimensions.

The main consciousness operating on our planet is still not raising up the energy to the heart and the higher chakras. This is why we miss so much love and compassion on Earth. Most of us have this energy potential dormant inside. It is called kundalini; an energy that lies dormant at the base of the spine until it is activated. Through the practice of yoga, kundalini can be channeled upward through the chakras in the process of spiritual awakening. With the blessing of an enlightened master it is believed that one can experience it with incredible force. But it can also happen spontaneously. The kundalini can rise in many different ways. It can be gentle and progressive or it can be sudden. There are no rules, but the body and mind must be prepared. This is the real meaning of yoga: a preparation for a meditation, in which we will raise this energy inside of us.

When we start to bring this energy up to the heart and the higher chakras, other dimensions of reality open up for us. Entering these dimensions transforms our reality, as we drop down all our theories and everything we thought we knew. We surrender completely and realize in truth we knew nothing, we are nothing. We are a humble part of the cosmic dream.

How can it fit in human consciousness that we are smaller than one grain of sand compared to the enormity of this universe? Yet we have an energy lying inside of us that can take us into a cosmic orgasm of pure ecstasy. The kundalini is pure Shakti energy, pure life force, power of creation. But one can only experience it when the channels of the chakras are open and flowing all the way up.

Shakti means "power" and is the divine feminine force personified in all expressions of the hindu mythology. She is the dynamic, primordial creative energy that supports life. Shakti is considered non-separate from Shiva, the Absolute Consciousness. This union is historically depicted in images of Ardhanārīśvara, the androgynous form of god who is half man, half woman. Here, Shiva and Shakti are consciousness and energy in an eternal dance of creation, sustainment, and dissolution.

Shakti is dynamic energy that is responsible for the creation, maintenance, and destruction of the universe. Shakti is responsible for creation, as mothers are responsible for birth. Without Shakti, nothing in this universe would happen; Shakti doesn't only give birth to the universe. She is the universe, from the minutest particle to the densest cosmic body. She veils herself in each of us when we fail to see our divine nature.

> *"Shakti is the potential for recognizing our true identity, she is kuṇḍalinī (the "coiled one"), which remains dormant but awakens in the context of deep yogic insight. Kuṇḍalinī is often depicted as a coiled serpent at the base of the spine, where she lies asleep until one experiences śaktipāta, which literally means the 'descent of śakti,' a bestowal of divine grace."*[2]
>
> *Elen Goldberg*

While considered feminine, Shakti is non-binary, being present in all beings, all genders, and all objects as their true nature. In other words, all attributes of reality are but the face of Shakti. She is the source, the expression, and the ultimate dissolution of anything and everything in existence. Since Shakti is everything in existence, she is invoked in all modes of spiritual practice. The divine mother, she is the power and source of mantra or sacred sound, yantra or sacred art, ritual worship, contemplative practices, and meditation. Shakti governs our spiritual evolution, opening up the inner world of meditation, and unfolding the state of union, or yoga, between body, mind and spirit. Shakti is our nature.

---

2 *The Lord Who is Half Woman: Ardhanārīśvara in Indian and Feminist Perspective*, Ellen Goldberg, SUNY Press, 2002.

When humans are locked in suffering, it is because the energy is blocked in the lower chakras. Indeed, suffering is also part of life. We do not deny suffering and darkness. It is the only way love and compassion can manifest. We have an energy generator inside of us; our solar plexus, which is always operating but not fully activated. If we don't activate and raise our energy, darkness will remain. But when activated, power from the source becomes unlimited. We bring light from inside and distribute this energy to the whole body, from the soles of the feet to the top of the head, and to our surroundings, families, communities, and everyone who comes in contact with us.

We can choose the intensity of the light, and the vibration we want to exist in.

One of my favourite quotes comes from Einstein:

> *"Everything is energy and that's all there is to it. Match the frequency of the reality you want, and you cannot help but get that reality. It can be no other way."*

Everything vibrates at its own frequency, yet it all comes from one source of energy. What appears to be solid matter is nothing more than vibrating energy. Your physical body is essentially a tool used for translation and has the ability to translate vibrations into physical experience. A physically translated manifestation is simply a specific frequency that has been laid upon itself so many times that it turns dense. When the frequency becomes strong enough due to the adequate mental energy, as visualization and belief, the physical senses can recognize it and translate it as a concrete, tangible thing.

There is an infinite number of frequencies vibrating with other things at similar frequencies. In the realm of our imagination and the nonphysical, things become real instantaneously, but in a way that is not physical. The mind has the ability to form new creations by piercing the limitations of the physical frequency in which it is currently held. In other words, stretching the vibration into other places triggers manifestation. This is the starting point; it's the place to begin if you want to move into new physical translations and realities. When the new vibrational frequency is maintained, it matches alike frequencies, and the physical senses will translate those new frequencies as the new reality.

This is why thought and imagination are so important. They are the catalysts for new experiences and new realities. You can sense certain things in your thoughts, although you don't see them yet in your physically perceived reality. This is because the frequency of your physical body hasn't caught up yet with what you are creating in your mind. The physical senses remain at their current frequency or the last frequency that you adjusted them to. Therefore, they can only continue streaming the sensory information that matches with that frequency range.

This is what makes the physical body so magnificent. It's an instrument that has the purpose of interpreting vibration into experiences for us. Because of the senses in our bodies, we are able to create different perceptions of sight, scent, touch, sound, and taste. Our physical bodies have their own frequency, and each individual's frequency creates their range of experience. There is a vibrational frequency at the root of everything we sense, and tuning ourselves is the true power source behind manifesting.

The Function of Chakras

In traditional Indian medicine and spiritual science, the physical body is more than merely bones, muscles, and organs encased in skin. Instead, it includes layers of energy fields that surround the physical body. These interconnected metaphysical layers create the body's electromagnetic field, also known as its aura. This is what's known as the subtle body, also referred to as the "light body," "etheric body," or "spiritual body."

In yoga, the life force energy (prana) travels through the subtle body in a series of channels, called nadis. These nadis intersect at points of intensified energy, called chakras. A Sanskrit word for wheel, chakras are spinning vortexes of energy in the subtle body that correspond to various glands along the spine and inside the skull.

Modern literature from both Western and Eastern cultures highlight the connection between the chakras and human biology. The endocrine system plays a major role in the body's daily health. The endocrine glands release hormones directly into the bloodstream and control every aspect of growth and development. Overall, our network of glands oversees the production, regulation, and distribution of hormones throughout the body. Hormones play a key role in the body's ability to mature, metabolize nutrients, and function properly.

Disturbances in the subtle energy of the chakras are translated into a physical manifestation through the corresponding glands and organs related to each chakra. Chakras influence our well-being at many levels: whenever one of our energy centers is thrown out of balance because of a blockage, physical symptoms may appear. The chakras distribute ki (also called chi, or prana) throughout the physical body. Most of us have energetic blocks and imbalances as well as energy-sabotaging habits that prevent us from accessing our full vitality, which leads us to feel exhausted, scattered, dull, or ill.

The chakras are located in alignment with the vertebrae and distribute the energy through our body. Each chakra is paired with an endocrine gland that governs its functionality. The endocrine glands are the connection between the energetic nature of the chakras and the physical functions of the body. Below, I will briefly list how the chakras and endocrine glands are paired and their respective Sanskrit name:

1. Root Chakra (Muladhara) — Reproductive glands (testicles in men; ovaries in women); controls sexual development and secretes sex hormones.
2. Sacral Chakra (Svadisthana) — Adrenal glands; regulates the immune system and metabolism.
3. Solar Plexus Chakra (Manipura) — Pancreas; regulates metabolism.
4. Heart Chakra (Anahata) — Thymus gland; regulates the immune system.
5. Throat Chakra (Vishuddi) — Thyroid gland; regulates body temperature and metabolism.
6. Third Eye Chakra (Ajna) — Pituitary gland; produces hormones and governs the function of the previous five glands;.
7. Crown Chakra (Sahasrara) — Pineal gland[3]; regulates biological cycles, including sleep.

In addition to each chakra governing one of the seven glands, there are seven major organs that are also related. Here is a list of each chakra and the organs it influences:

- Root — Testicles, ovaries, kidneys, spine

3 The pineal gland is linked to the third eye chakra as well as to the crown chakra. The pituitary gland and the pineal gland are the two chakra glands that serve to regulate overall glandular and biological function of the body. The pituitary's main function is to regulate body chemistry. Located between the eyes, this pea-sized gland regulates emotion and intellect, and works in partnership with the pineal gland to achieve overall balance. Essentially, the cone-shaped pineal gland governs and (when necessary) inhibits pituitary gland function.

- Sacral — Bladder, prostate, ovaries, kidneys, gallbladder, bowel, spleen
- Solar Plexus — Intestines, pancreas, liver, bladder, stomach, upper spine
- Heart — Heart, lungs
- Throat — Bronchial tubes, vocal cords, respiratory system, all areas of the mouth, including tongue and oesophagus.
- Third Eye — Eyes, pituitary and pineal glands, brain
- Crown — Spinal cord and brainstem

Chakras and Colors

The chakra system is also related to colors. A journey through the seven chakras is essentially a journey through the rainbow. Each of your seven chakras has a corresponding color that follows the colors of the rainbow: red, orange, yellow, green, blue, indigo, and violet (or white).

Color is a universal language and provides us with a mirror for our emotions. It is very simple and yet very profound. Colors are actually waves traveling through space, and our eyes register different colors depending on the wavelength, the space between the peaks (measured in nanometers nm).

The vibratory rate of a substance determines its density or its form as matter. A slowly vibrating substance is referred to as physical matter, whereas the subatomic (which vibrates at or above the speed of light) is subtle matter or pure light energy. Light is electromagnetic radiation, which is the fluctuation of electric and magnetic fields in nature. More simply, light is energy, and the phenomenon of color is a product of the interaction of energy and matter. The wavelength, frequency, and quantity of energy of every colorful ray are fixed for each color; that is, a specific wavelength, a certain frequency, and a particular amount of energy in that wave has been denominated to a distinct color. The human eye is sensitive to electromagnetic radiation only at limited wavelengths. This small segment is called the visible spectrum; this visible light can be broken down into numerous electromagnetic frequencies. Each frequency relates to a color of the rainbow and relates to different levels of consciousness.

We see and recognize color when photons enter the retina, where they are transformed into electrical impulses. These impulses reach the brain through electrochemical reactions in the nerve cells. The brain then transfers these reactions into the pictures that we "see" in our minds and then project outside of our bodies. The process of seeing and recognizing a color occurs within ourselves and is projected outwards.

The color red has the longest wavelength, while at the other end of the spectrum is violet, with the smallest wavelength. The visible light spectrum is part of the electromagnetic spectrum and its wavelengths range between approximately 380-740 nm.

Each of your chakras is vibrating at a particular frequency and responds to different vibrations (or wavelengths) of light. Within these frequencies and wavelengths, each color contains information on several different levels: physical, mental, emotional, and spiritual.

All this wisdom about chakras has been used in yoga for thousands of years. We can regulate the function of the chakras by practicing yoga, breathwork, pranayama, meditation, relaxation or visualization techniques, in addition to physical exercises and a balanced diet.

There is so much to be said about chakras, but I will keep it simple. Understanding the correlation between your energetic flow and your health is what really matters. We all want to be healthy, and if we learn some simple meditation techniques, it can increase and open up our energetic system, allowing us to experience different levels of our existence and, consequently, the experiences we are creating in our lives. We can use simple meditation practices to optimize our energetic system, to heal and open the flow in our chakras, and unleash the full power of the life force within us.

Sunshine on You

We can use the light and energy of the sun for our benefit in a conscious and practical way. Sunbath therapy is also a natural way of keeping us healthy and of healing different health problems. Sunlight helps to regulate melatonin production in the body, which is necessary for maintaining our circadian rhythms. Melatonin is the essential hormone released by our pineal gland which regulates our sleep-wake cycle, directly affected by the intensity of sunlight. It increases during the night and falls during the daytime. Depriving ourselves of healthy exposure to the sun also causes deficiency of vitamin D in the body.

It has been found that decreased exposure to sunlight may lead to physical and psychological disorders. In such a fast, speedy, busy, modern and artificial lifestyle we are usually not exposed to as much sunlight as we naturally should be. It is very important to expose ourselves to sun rays in a healthy way. But we should not sunbathe in very strong sunlight because then it can become harmful. The intensity of the sun should be comfortable; it should not make you sweat or burn your skin.

Vitamin D deficiency is a global public health issue, and not many people are aware of this. About 1 billion people worldwide have a vitamin D deficiency, while 50% of the population has vitamin D insufficiency. A low vitamin D status is emerging as a very common condition worldwide, and several studies from basic science to clinical applications have highlighted a strong association with chronic diseases, as well as acute conditions. The status worldwide indicates this subclinical vitamin D deficiency is associated with osteoporosis, increased risk of falls and fragility fractures. Many recent studies are now showing an association between vitamin D deficiency and cancer, cardiovascular disease, diabetes, autoimmune diseases, and depression.

About 50% to 90% of vitamin D is absorbed through the skin via sunlight while the rest comes from the diet. Twenty minutes of sunshine daily with over 40% of skin exposed is required to prevent vitamin D deficiency. Cutaneous synthesis of vitamin D declines with aging. We might need more exposure to the sun, to pay attention to our diet or to take a supplement. But be aware that high doses of vitamin D can be harmful to the body and cause hypervitaminosis D and hypercalcemia. Although vitamin D has been used as an alternative treatment for many sicknesses, in higher doses it should be taken only under the supervision of a doctor for a specific treatment.

Dark-skinned people also have less cutaneous vitamin D synthesis. Decreased exposure to the sun as seen in individuals who are institutionalized, and prolonged hospitalizations can also lead to vitamin D deficiency. Effective sun exposure is decreased in individuals who use sunscreen consistently. We might think we are protecting our skin when we use sunscreen but vitamin D is very important for health and we need to be aware of how to best use sun protection.

The functioning of the human body is impossible without maintaining an energetic continuum driven by sunlight. The sun and seven major chakras existing over the spinal cord help maintain this energetic continuum.

During my time in the Philippines, I heard about an alternative Filipino doctor; the friend of my teacher Pi Villaraza, called Dr. Romy Paredes. He is one of the world's many catalysts for the vision quest for a new health care system—the ultimate healthcare system. Author of seven books and founder of Self Health Empowerment Movement, a non-profit organization with the mission of empowering people to take control of their health, Dr. Paredes has an unusual way of treating his patients. His system is based on self health education, and self-health empowerment to bring back the glory of the divine design of human beings. Dr. Paredes prescribes lots of sunlight, exercise, drinking water, nature walks and a balanced light diet to support the lifestyle changes of people who are sick or aiming to keep healthy. In truth, this is mainly what we need: a system that bolsters people's sense of their own divine magnificence and returns them to the original state of love.

Colors and Emotions

Light and colors can influence the way we feel and react to different situations. Color can help to heal, energize, and soothe us. Colors can help correct physiological and psychological imbalances in the human body.

> *"You realize you are part of the hologram of life, surrounded by an aura or energy field that radiates distinct colour and vibrations. The aura fingertips your soul and reflects your goodness, wellness, mental stability, maturity, emotional/inner turmoil or peaceful fulfilment. More of each of these qualities, peace, wellness, stability, maturity and fulfilment may become your ever present precious possession by the application of colour's power in our daily living"*
> *Walker M. in Power of Colours.*

In the spectrum of colors of the rainbow related to the chakras, the color red embodies our root chakra. It influences emotional issues like financial independence and physical survival. Red orange may also produce similar effects. It's mostly used for physical healing because its emotional effects can be extreme. Avoid shining red light on the head, as this can cause intense agitation. Neither red nor infrared should be used for someone who has severe mental conditions.

Orange relates to the sacral chakra. It brings abundance, action, pleasure, and well-being. It can be used to stimulate different organs in the human body for physical healing, as it revitalizes and gives you increased mental energy. It also increases the feeling of connectedness between your mind and body. However, orange is not recommended for anxiety.

Yellow, related to our solar plexus, can be used in color therapy to bring energy and encourage action. This color can make you feel happier. It can bring out your intelligence and wisdom. It can also remind us of our mortality. Yellow is the most intense color in the spectrum.

Green represents the heart chakra. Interacting with green plants is also a natural way to ease stress. When you're feeling sad, hopeless, or depressed, green can improve your mood. Green can enhance the emotions of love, joy, and inner peace. It can bring you hope, strength, and serenity. Green is said to increase your wisdom and facilitate change and independence.

Blue embodies the throat chakra. It is a color that helps you express your feelings and thoughts, and is related to your inner truth. It helps you become more peaceful and relaxed. Blue light can be used to focus on tranquillity. Primary blue is often used in therapy settings for meditation and relaxation. It is associated with wisdom, creativity, loyalty, and spirituality. Light blue promotes serenity and it can help insomnia. However, it is not recommended for depression.

For example, if you're having trouble focusing or staying alert, take a walk outside where you can get plenty of natural blue light. At night, however, blue light can cause us harm by disrupting our biological clocks, or circadian rhythms. This is because it suppresses melatonin, the hormone that helps our bodies sleep. Turn your phone and computer off several hours before bed to keep their blue light from interfering with your circadian rhythm. There's also software that can help with this, like Flux. Flux changes the color of your computer's light depending on the time of day, triggering warm colors at night and sunlight colors in the daytime. If you need a nightlight, you can use dim red lights.

The third eye chakra, located between the eyebrows, is represented by indigo and associated with the pituitary gland and pineal gland, and influences our sleep cycles, self-esteem, clarity, wisdom, and intuition.

Violet, at the crown chakra, is most strongly associated with beauty, spirituality, and bliss. In color therapy, violet is often used on the forehead and neck to initiate feelings of calm and relaxation within the human body. However, it's also recommended for use on any part of the body. The crown chakra, located at the top of the head, is associated with the pineal gland, light sensitivity, sleep cycles, dreams, clarity, and spirituality.

Warm colors are useful in arousing those troubled with reactive depression or neurasthenia. They have been shown to increase muscle tone or blood pressure in hypertensive individuals. Cool colors elicited the reverse affective responses. Anxious subjects were actually calmed by these cooler colors. Cool colors can be effective as a tranquilizer in cases of tension and anxiety. Physiologically, all colors produce clinically tangible results. Exposure to warm colors increases respiratory movements, frequency of eye blinks, cortical activation and palmar conductance (arousal of the autonomic nervous system). Warm colors consistently show a more pronounced pattern of stimulation. Cool colors have the opposite effects by acting as a relaxant and tranquilizer for anxious individuals, lowering blood pressure, providing relief from tension, alleviating muscle spasms, and reducing eye blink frequency. They have also proved to be an aid for insomnia. Just as warm colors showed a consistently pronounced pattern of stimulation, cool colors showed a consistent pattern of relaxation.

Scanning the Chakras

Understanding the chakras system is simple, yet incredibly powerful. You can learn how to harness life-force energy to support you, your emotional well-being, and the whole system of your body. The subtle body is basically an intricate energetic system. There are different levels of consciousness in the spiritual realm, and that is where the chakra system comes into play.

Inspired by some practices of yoga, I have a simple yogic philosophy I adapted to suit my own way. Basically, it is a sequence of affirmations, functioning as a prayer for each of the chakras.

We know we have seven main chakras, each related to a certain endocrine gland. Our chakras are related to the production of hormones and, so, to our emotions, in a curious way.

The first chakra is basically our connection with Mother Earth, nature, our roots, and our sexuality. The second chakra also, but it expresses pure creativity. The third chakra adds pure satisfaction. If you want to know how well your energy is flowing or how blocked it is, check on your first three chakras. Look at your connection with Mother Earth, with the elements, with nature, at your sexuality, your creativity, and your level of satisfaction in life.

From the third chakra, the natural energy flow rises up to the heart chakra—the fourth energy center—where love and compassion awaken. When the lower chakras are working well, the energy naturally flows up to the heart. This is when we experience pure love, understanding, and compassion.

From the heart, the energy flows up to the throat, the fifth chakra, where love, freedom, and your inner truth are expressed freely, through your voice. At this point, if the energy is flowing, only sweetness and loving words can come out. Any aggression simply fades away. Loving communication expands, and a deep sense of collectiveness emerges.

If energy keeps flowing and rising, it goes up to our third eye, the pituitary gland, home of the sixth chakra. It is the place of the present moment, this sacred moment—the gift of now. The third eye chakra allows us to truly feel centered and to experience a pristine balance between all polarities, between the two sides of our brain, right and left hemispheres, between our intellect and intuition, yin and yang, feminine and masculine energies, past and future, and so on.

Lastly, the energy flows to the crown chakra on the top of our heads, our pineal gland. It is the seventh chakra, where we reach a state of union with all life. A sense of interdependence and understanding comes in and through us, and we experience pure consciousness and an overflow of love. We start to experience love everywhere and in everything. All is love, all is one, and one contains all.

Through the emotion-related aspects of our chakras, we can have a clearer idea about how we are doing energetically; how blocked and how flowing our chakras are. It is very simple. Just ask yourself: how pure and innocent am I? How is my connection to Earth? How do I touch Mother Earth and the process of life? How is my relation to the ground under my feet? How do I walk on Earth? Do I walk in peace and gratitude? (first chakra)

Now, check: how is your creativity level in life? Are you re-inventing yourself? Are you creating new solutions, new possibilities, new ways of thinking? Are you using your artistic talents to express yourself? (second chakra)

Now, ask yourself, how is your level of satisfaction? Can you find satisfaction in the most simple things in life? Or have you been experiencing anger, stress, negative emotions and so many countless desires? (third chakra)

If you want to know how blocked or how open you are in your first three energy centers, just ask yourself these questions: How much understanding, compassion and love are you experiencing? Are you holding on to any pain from the past, or fears about the future? How much do you trust yourself and this divine intelligence that created life? (heart chakra)

Are you able to express and share your love to others in a collective manner? Are you speaking the truth of your heart? How much sweetness is coming out of your voice? Can you still use your voice to hurt others? How do you use your voice? Have you been smoking? (throat chakra, thyroid gland)

Go further and ask yourself: How deep can you forgive yourself and others? Are you conscious and living in the present moment? Are you feeling centered and balanced? (third eye, pituitary gland)

Are you experiencing union with all living beings and creatures on Earth? How do you understand yourself as part of life, in communion and non-separation? (sahastrara, pineal gland)

As we answer all these questions, we find out that the level of consciousness on our planet is still very blocked in the lower chakras. Mass consciousness is blocked and vibrating basically in the lower chakras. Very few people are consciously raising the energy, with their heart open. That is why there is so much sickness on our planet. In reality, we came out of primitivism not long ago, and our civilization has created technology that gives us the illusion that we are advanced in our understanding of life and the energy systems inside ourselves. But the energy in our bodies is still very blocked. This energy is just waiting to be seen, to be felt, to be spoken and to be raised up so we might experience our divine potential as human beings.

The true reason for sickness is that most of us are energetically blocked in our lower chakras. We have lost our connection with Mother Earth and our true nature. We have lost our purity and innocence. We have lost our creativity, with an education system that does not foster freedom, imagination and originality. To add insult to injury, our sexuality has also been manipulated to equate it to mere sensual pleasure. The divine sexual energy—the innocence and beauty of it—is predominantly lost.

Very few of us are consciously cleaning and cleansing ourselves from inside, we believe it is enough to clean the physical body, to take a shower, but we are not deep cleaning our mind and energetic body.

We must open the internal system of the chakras, to allow this energy to flow up to the heart and upper chakras. This is our energetic system, and when it is blocked, eventually the body and mind becomes sick. Balance your chakras, raise this energy within yourself, and the divine light will shine all around you!

10. INTO PRACTICE

In this chapter, you can find simple practices available to all, which can reduce stress, increase calmness and clarity, and promote happiness. Learning how to meditate is straightforward, and the benefits can come quickly. You can get started on a path toward greater equanimity, acceptance and joy. Take a deep breath, and get ready to relax.

Once we have crossed the river, we can let go of the raft; we have reached the other side of the river. We can even let go of all the theories; and just live with the practice. Our practice is what is most important. All theories, ideas, concepts, and philosophies are just like a boat that we use to cross to the other side. Once we have understood and reached the other side, we can let it go.

I am the kind of person that likes to go all in. I am going to go deep with you, to penetrate the realms of the unknown, of our true nature. Let's take action now, acknowledging how energy affects the individual and the collective through our own practice.

Even just a few minutes of meditation can make a big difference when practiced regularly. The purpose of meditation is to become mindful, conscious throughout all parts of our life, so that we're awake, present, and open-hearted in everything we do.

There are many spiritual traditions and forms of meditation. I will share with you simple and effective methods I have been practicing over the years. They include elements and influences of Vipassana (or insight) meditation from Burmese Theravada Buddhist tradition, mantra from bhakti devotional practice, yogic, and metta meditation.

These are all beautiful ways to support awareness practices. They reconnect us to life, some specific words and phrases can evoke a boundless warm-hearted feeling. The strength of this feeling is not limited to or by family, religion, or social class; we begin with ourselves and gradually extend the wish for well-being and happiness to all beings. May we use mindfulness of breath and all modern and ancient teachings as tools to nourish and experience heaven on Earth.

It reminds me a story of a westerner who once arrived at an ashram in India and asked how to meditate. Maharaj-ji, the guru, suddenly became silent and closed his eyes for a few breaths. When a tear trickled down his cheek, he answered: "Meditate the way Christ meditated. Christ lost himself in pure Love. He lives in the hearts of all beings. In truth, he never died. He never died." The message is very clear: lose yourself in love.

Chakra Meditation & Connection with Earth

This meditation is an easy and practical way to apply the ancient knowledge of the chakras to our lives. It is a kind of prayer meditation, using affirmations. Remember that every time we affirm something, we are building up a reality inside ourselves—we reinforce it to become true for us. What we give to life, life gives back to us. We experience this every day, but we may not recognize that it is happening.

I recommend you read this section first and then try the exercises outlined within it. If you feel you need to write something down as a reminder, until you memorize it, feel free.

We want to heal ourselves, so let's first reconnect with the Earth from within. This connection is our root chakra. We will raise our energy up with the help of Mother Earth, who supports our existence in all senses from the moment we are born. We will cleanse and raise the energy, chakra by chakra. And we will use certain affirmations to help and guide the mind.

Remember: meditation is more about feelings and observation, it is not so much about the technique. It truly happens only when it comes from your heart. Meditation has existed for thousands of years, from the birth of our civilization. There is nothing to worry about, just trust your breath. Trust that your next breath will be there for you.

Feel love in everything you do, or you will be misusing your time and energy on this planet. The most important thing is to connect with your heart. Feeling joy while meditating means you are practicing the right way.

The practice:

Make sure you sit in a quiet place, in a room or in nature, where you will not be disturbed. You can sit comfortably barefoot, on the ground or on a chair. With your spine straightened, close your eyes. Feel the contact with the Earth underneath you, whether it is the floor, grass, or a sandy beach, does not matter. The important thing here is to connect and feel Mother Earth inside of you. Feel this connection with Earth and all the elements within you.

Use your right hand to touch the earth directly, by your side. Alternatively, you can just visualize it. Feel how everything belongs to and returns to

Earth. Picture how even our bodies will return to Earth one day. Feel how Mother Earth is supporting, nourishing, and caring for you all the time.

Now, bring your attention to the base of your spine, to the sacral area under your genitals, the meeting point between your legs. Feel this space, your first energy center, known as Muladhara. Feel this space on the base of your spine. As you deepen your connection, touch the Earth and feel you are not separated from it. Earth and all the elements are inside of you, me, and all of us. Feel Mother Earth's generosity, love, and support. Consciously, you are giving everything back to the Earth. Through this contact and connection, feel the cleansing of any blockages you might have at this first chakra and energy center, and in your energetic field.

Breathing in and out deeply, feel the elements within you. Consciously, breathe the air, sense your lungs and all the cells of your body nourished by it. Feel the water within you, the sacred water from the veins of the earth. Feel the sun, the great generator, the source of energy and fire inside you. Feel the ground and how it supports, nourishes, and gives you all the nutrients you need to survive. Feel how you are connected to all the elements.

It also includes a sexuality that is bright and beautiful, like a clean, pure, source of water. Here we are reconnecting to Earth, to our natural state of being—our true being—and letting creative energy expand our potential.

Feel how Mother Earth is helping you clean all the negativity stockpiled in your root chakra. Any negativity—conscious or unconscious—that might block your energy is now being released. Any kind of blockage at this energy center is returning to the Earth. All blockages can be released through this connection, this acceptance, this release. Earth has the power to heal it all and to purify.

Now, repeat these words internally:

Please, Mother Earth, let me return to innocence, to a pure state of mind, and to the divine within me.

Repeat it as many times you feel necessary. In this way, you are cleansing your first chakra.

Now, let's go up, bringing this energy to your second chakra, Svadhisthana. It is your sacral chakra, a few inches up your spine, just below your navel. Visualize this energy rising through your spine. Give back to Earth any kind of blockages in your second energy center, remembering how everything belongs and returns to Mother Earth.

You are inviting creativity back to your system to experience a state of mind that includes everything. We want to return to innocence and enjoy all of life's beauty. Repeat the affirmation below a few times, or however many times you feel necessary to deepen your connection between your second chakra and the Earth:

Please, Mother Earth, let me return to innocence, to a creative state of mind, and to the divine within me.

Repeat it as many times you feel necessary, cleansing your second chakra.

Now, bring the energy up to your third center, to your navel, your solar plexus: the Manipura chakra. There, you can feel a place of deep transformation and energy within you: your digestive system. It is where you transform all you eat into energy, and at the end, there is a letting go process, which takes your waste through your intestines. All that does not serve you must go out of your system and return to Earth.

Energetically, at this place there is a void, a black hole in which you can get caught; an ocean of illusion to cross, where all kinds of negative emotions (*vrittis* in Sanskrit) gather. The third chakra is the energy generator of your body, related to your level of satisfaction: physically, emotionally and spiritually. To know if your energy is flowing well at this energy center, look at your levels of satisfaction in life. The more it flows, the more satisfied you are with the simple things.

As you continue to feel and touch Mother Earth with your hand, visualize that you are returning to Earth anything that might be blocking your third chakra from flowing freely. This powerful energy center is your source of light; the sun and the fire inside of you. Anything that might be blocking your third chakra, any kind of negativity and blockages, you can now release. The affirmation here is:

Please, Mother Earth, let me be a more and more satisfied person; to experience pure satisfaction with everything, and all simple things.

Repeat it as many times as you feel necessary, cleansing your third chakra.

Now, bring this energy up to your heart chakra, Anahata. Once again, imagine that you are returning to Earth any kind of negativity, anything that might be blocking your energy from flowing freely to your heart. Earth is cleansing. Visualize that you are releasing all your fears and pain from the past. Those memories are not the truth of your soul. Your past is not your truth unless you choose to keep it alive. Your truth can only exist in the present moment. It is all we truly have. Everything else is just memories, stored data, blockages in your system.

It's very important here to make sure you release all your pain and fears from the past and give them back to the Earth. You do not need to keep any more pain and fear in your system; instead, you can be free. Release it, opening your heart, and receiving the support, love and generosity from Mother Earth in return. When this energy is flowing well, you will no longer experience pain and fear. Instead, you experience pure love and compassion. This energy can now flow freely up to your heart, creating a space of trust and surrender to the Universe.

The affirmation here is:

Please, Mother Earth, let me experience pure love, compassion, and understanding for myself and all living beings and creatures.

Repeat it as many times as you feel necessary, cleansing your fourth chakra.

Next, bring this feeling to your throat chakra, Visuddha. Feel it rise through your throat and give to the Earth anything that might be blocking it from flowing freely. Earth is a loving mother; she takes it all back. All blockages and negativity in this energy center can return to Mother Earth now.

When this energy is flowing well, your voice is full of sweetness. No longer will you speak in an aggressive manner or hurt anyone with your words. Love comes out in the form of gentle sounds. A sense of collectiveness arises and we want to share the love that is coming up from our hearts with every living being. As you feel this energy rising, just bend your elbows and raise your hands near your shoulders, turn your wrists, palms facing backwards, imagine creating a shape like a chimney. In this position, repeat the affirmation:

Please, Mother Earth, let only sweetness come through my voice, and let the love I am feeling in my heart express itself freely in all directions.

Repeat it as many times as you feel necessary, cleansing your fifth chakra.

After repeating this a few times, put both hands back on your knees and bring this energy up to your third eye chakra, Ajna, in the center of your forehead, your source of wisdom. As you breathe the beautiful air in and out, feel this energy center, and sense a total balance between the two sides of your brain. There is a balance between the right and left hemisphere: masculine and feminine, yin and yang, and all polarities in life.

At this point, you are in balance between the past and the future. When energy flows to your third eye, you fully experience the gift of the present moment—what truly belongs to you. In this space, you are able to forgive, experiencing the highest state of love. Forgiveness is a gift that you give to yourself and to the entire planet. The affirmation here is:

Please, Mother Earth, let me be able to forgive everyone and everything, including myself.

Repeat this however many times you feel is necessary to deepen your connection and sense of forgiveness. Keep your focus on the present moment, feel the truth of forgiveness in your heart. Feel this energy moving into your third eye, from the base of the spine up to your pituitary gland.

From here, bring the energy to the top of your head, your crown chakra, the Sahasrara, the pineal gland. Feel that you are not separated from anything, but rather united and part of everything. Imagine you are a drop of water, becoming one with the entire ocean. Simply stay there, in this state. You can choose to be in your third eye longer, but if you already have forgiven everything, you might like to go to the top of your head and unite with all living beings and creatures, and with the entire universe. You can feel this breath of life, allowing this feeling to integrate inside your body, mind, and heart.

Feel this ocean of love. The love that has always been there. There is no separation when you reach this space. We are all one. The entire universe is within us. We are the universe. In each breath, we are aware. Feel this expansion, and keep your focus on your breath for as long as you wish. Experience the feeling of each breath.

This is an extremely powerful meditation technique that anyone can practice. By doing it regularly, and with the help of Mother Earth, we can clean up all the blockages in our energy centers. The more we do it, the more this energy will flow throughout our bodies, and we will experience wholeness at an emotional, spiritual, and physical level.

Once, I did this meditation on top of a mountain called Panchasi, in Nepal. I woke up to see the sunrise in a remote village, just absorbed by the beauty of the Himalayas. I closed my eyes, connected with Earth and my breath, with all my heart. When

I opened my eyes, nearly six hours had passed; the sun was already high in the sky. I had entered a state of no time and space. Meditation can make us have this kind of experience. This showed me how powerful this simple meditation can be. It is just about going deeper and deeper into the heart. We all have this capacity.

Ho'oponopono

For me, Ho'oponopono meditation contains everything in a very simple and powerful way, and contains basically all that we need to practice.

The word ho'o means cause in Hawaiian, while ponopono means perfection. The repetition of the word pono means doubly right. or being right with both self and others. In a nutshell, ho'oponopono is a process by which we can nurture gratitude, love and forgiveness. This practice is very simple and powerful for purifying one's body, such as cleansing memories and feelings that hold the mind in a negative tune.

> *"Have you heard of Ho'oponopono and the Hawaiian therapist who cured an entire ward of criminally insane patients, without ever meeting any of them or spending a moment in the same room? It's not a joke. The therapist was Dr. Ihaleakala Hew Len."*
> *Joe Vitale*

What if we realize that our biggest illusion is that we believe things are happening outside of ourselves? And that from inside we can access everyone and everything—just from inside ourselves.

Ho'oponopono is an ancient Hawaiian practice of self-healing, brought to the modern-day by Dr. Hew Len, a clinical psychologist who worked in Hawaii State Hospital and helped heal an entire ward of mentally ill criminals. The way he did this was by first reviewing each patient's file and then performing the Ho'oponopono to himself. The results were miraculous: he was able to heal the patients by healing himself.

This story comes from bestselling author Joe Vitale. Whether it is true or not, I decided to practice Ho'oponopono because of its content. And the outcome I had with this practice was immense.

Ho'oponopono questions the common mindset which draws a distinction between a subjective inner world and an objective outside world. It breaks the paradigms of separation. We can access everyone and everything from inside of ourselves. No problem or situation ever happens outside of ourselves, but is all coming from inside. In order for this practice to work, we first must take responsibility for everything and every situation in our lives. We need courage to take all responsibility, to understand that, energetically speaking, we attract and create all our experiences.

Simply by repetition of the words: *Thank you; I love you; I am sorry; please, forgive me,* we are addressing the divine Intelligence that governs us and all life. We are cleaning our system from the inside, and opening access to all stored data coming from the unconscious mind and from our ancestors.

During many years of personal practice with this method, my results have been astounding. We have the power to change not only our life circumstances but any complicated situations around us. We have the ability to bring so much love, gratitude and forgiveness into ourselves. Practicing Ho'oponopono heals our environment and those around us. It is a continuous journey of self-discovery, of diving deep into love, forgiveness and gratitude—all we truly need. In fact, life is an experience that unravels from the inside out. If we really start to do the work inside ourselves, we can harness the power to transform our surroundings, and the entire planet, because in truth we are all connected.

You might wonder why or how repeating such words affects anything "out there." The secret is: "out there" does not exist; everything happens to you in your mind. All that you see, everything you hear, every person you meet, is an experience within your mind. If you think it's only "out there," you mistakenly believe you are absolved of responsibility. In fact, it's quite the opposite: you are responsible for everything you think and that happens to you, even if you don't understand how you have attracted everything you experience into your energy field. If you watch the news, everything "out there" becomes your responsibility. That may sound overwhelming, but you are also able to clear it, clean it, and through forgiveness, you can change it.

The practice of Ho'oponopono promotes self-awareness, emotional stability, and compassion. The good news is that you can do this process by yourself. All you have to do is repeat the words in your head. The power is in the feeling and in the natural order of how our universe is designed. Ho'oponopono invites you to tune in to the frequency of gratitude, love and forgiveness. It embraces everything; the essence of all religions and teachings of all masters. And miracles start to happen. What a wonderful dream of a planet where love, gratitude and forgiveness are everywhere!

Do you need a miracle? How can this possibly work? How can you heal yourself and simultaneously heal others? How can you even heal yourself?

All you need to do is to internally repeat four mantras as if you were running a cleansing program in your operational system. When doing this, you are simply addressing the divine energy that is everywhere and in everything. Focus continuously on the mantras: "Thank you. I love you. I am sorry. Please forgive me." Just trust and keep repeating them internally, allowing miracles to happen in your life! You can do this while sitting, lying down, walking, or doing any other work. Just repeat the mantras inside of you, and go deeper into your own heart.

Applying Ho'oponopono

"To understand everything is to forgive everything."
Osho

Ho'oponopono asks the Universe for forgiveness, which is essential for our liberation. We ask for forgiveness not only for ourselves but for all of humanity and our ancestors. We ask forgiveness for our ignorance, our limited vision and perception, for all that is happening inside and outside of us, and for our mistakes and lack of understanding in our past and present. So, repeat with me:

I am sorry. Please, forgive me.

Sometimes we feel so small, and we lack understanding of our suffering and the suffering of others. If I was not able to pay proper attention before, or my vision was blurred, I can recognize it now and say to this divine energy:

I am sorry. Please forgive me.

Once, I had my eyes open and I looked at the beauty that surrounded me. I stared at the mountains and spoke to them as if they could hear me. I am part of humanity and I am a child of Earth. I knew Mother Earth and the Universe could hear me, and I told them:

Please, give me some of your strength and courage to share my deepest feelings.
I want to open up my heart to truly forgive myself and everyone around me,
And also to forgive my ancestors.
I am sorry. Please, forgive me.

Divine energy has the power to clean everything that needs to be cleaned, shining pure light and spreading seeds of love. We can water those seeds in us and step out of the darkness of the soul. We have so much pain and sorrow that we often struggle to understand ourselves. Most of us were not taught how to bring light and raise this energy flow into our hearts. We need more compassion for ourselves and for Mother Earth. I then said to this divine energy:

Thank you so much. Thank you for everything.

When practicing this meditation, beautiful tears of gratitude often flow from my eyes. Tears full of thankfulness, love, and compassion. For this Earth I give tears of joy, to nourish the soil of the collective soul. I am so grateful for Mother Earth's generosity, for holding beautiful oceans and forests, for nurturing us with so many delicious fruits and vegetables, for the fresh water and for the air that we breathe. How could I give back to Earth what

Earth has given to me? Breathe out this immense gratitude, saying internally:

I love you, I love you so much. I have seen so much beauty in you.
You have been nourishing us all the time.
I am breathing this air, this pure air.
I am breathing love from you, from millions of years of your existence, from all the trees.
Spirit of the mountain,
Spirit of the sea,
Spirit of the water,
Spirit of the fire,
Spirit of the sun,
Spirit of the wind...

Breathe. Keep breathing and pay close attention to it. We amplify the frequency of consciousness and then send these frequencies to far distances so they can reach more and more people around the globe. Love frequencies are not constrained to time and space. We are supported by many angels; we are not alone. Who knows how long we will be alive for? Don't waste your precious time. Go out, look at the sky with open arms, breathe and feel the sun and the light coming in. Just as you feel your breath, you can feel the sun. We can feel this energy coming from the air we breathe and the sun in our hearts.

We have the potential to bring love and light to millions of people. We are cosmic revolutionaries, and we came here for this reason. We do not want to waste time or the opportunity to protect life and beauty. We are warriors of the light! We do not want to feel sad or weak. We have planted the seed, taken care of it, and it has grown stronger. Soon the tree of life will give us fruits, and everyone will be able to eat them. What we plant we harvest, and you will be complete and fulfilled. When we connect with the abundance of our nature, it brings us the sweetest fruits.

We possess such advanced technology that has the capacity to multiply our energy in an exponential way. Just as we can go deep inside an atom to break it, we can go inside our own mind and create a new version of ourselves. It is the idea of self that we need to break, that is, our ego. If you understand how to break the illusion of self—the notion of ego—and go deep into the present moment, a bomb of energy will explode in your heart.

This is how energy works. Break up with everything you're attached to and let it go. Do not be afraid, for only the ego can feel fear. The soul does not have fear because it is pure love. Enjoy the adventure of being human, and soon you will learn to experience energy as you have never imagined.

You are amazing.
You are infinite.
You are all the universe.
Pure love and compassion.
And you are not your shadows.

We cannot get rid of our shadows, but we can laugh. Because we know our shadow is not who we truly are; it is not the real you. The real you is, ultimately, the person that creates the shadow and perceives it. If we try to rationalize everything in the mind, we lose our freedom of expression, the ultimate authenticity, honesty, and transparency. Do not be trapped by the darkness of your shadow.

If you do not yet understand this level of awareness, just let it be. Focus on the direction of your goals and soon you will dance hand in hand with life. Even your shadow will follow you. Dance baby, dance! Feel your divine soul, connect with the right frequency, and nothing will ever stop you from living your dreams. Just be. Just do it. And do not forget to enjoy each moment as a precious treasure!

I love you.
I love you, Mother Earth.
Thank you for those moments of appreciation.
Thank you for being with us and for taking care of us.
Thank you. I love you.

BREATH

We can make life simple, and make peace and happiness accessible for ourselves and for all of humanity. Let us get started right now by observing our breath. I invite you to breathe with me. Let us take a few breaths together consciously. Everything starts and ends with one breath. This is how we are born and how we will die. There is something very deep in our breath. Just by observing our breath, we can create more peace inside ourselves. It is the air coming into our body, our brain, and our lungs that creates our special connection to life. Breathing also allows the cells in our body to recharge and rejuvenate. The more we practice observing our breath, the more we will be able to go into this magical world inside ourselves.

Let us be aware of our breathing for a moment, taking a few breaths to connect with each other. Feel your breath coming in and going out of your body. Close your eyes and feel your nostrils, chest, and abdomen moving in and out with each breath. Inhale deeply, exhale slowly. Smile, and release. Breathe in peace for yourself and for the whole universe, feeling it in your body and spirit. It does not matter how close or far away we are from each other; by breathing together, we are connected. This is the connection of the heart. It is not limited to time and space. It is not an internet connection, it is a heart connection. If you need to focus your attention more, say internally "in" with each inhalation and "out" with each exhalation. *In. Out.* Do this a few times, until you feel totally present and aware of this moment.

Now, release all tension, and notice how your breath calms your brain activity. Just observe any thoughts that come through your mind, but let them go. Let it all go; the past and all memories stored in your mind. We want to free ourselves, don't we? Aren't we tired of having all this garbage blocking the energy flow in our bodies? Just try a few more deep breaths as you continue to read. With a sense of gratitude for your eyes, feel the air go through your nostrils, into your lungs, and to all the cells of your body. Bless the air you breathe!

Bring your attention to the present moment, to the here and now, and become one with your breath. This is a wonderful way to get in touch with your true nature, connecting with each other and with life. Just take a few deep breaths, extend them naturally and build inner peace with each inhalation and exhalation. It is important to let breathing happen naturally, without forcing it. Just observe the breath and what is happening right now. It is very easy and simple; you do not need to complicate things.

This is where your path starts.

The awakening of the spirit happens in accordance with the awakening of this breath of life. It happens when we connect with and observe our breath consciously. If we manage to have one breath in peace, we are also able to have three, four, five or however many breaths we want. As we rebuild inner peace, we restore our natural state of being.

Vipassana & Mindfulness

The focus of vipassana and mindfulness sitting meditation is the breath, following it and sharpening concentration (anapanna) can bring you incredible benefits. It is about bringing you right here, now, through the breath. You are alive! Breathing in and breathing out all the time.

All you need is to sit comfortably, with your back straight, head, neck, and chest aligned. Take a few slow, deep breaths, and close your eyes. Focus on the movement of your breath as it goes in and comes out of your body. Chose where to focus your attention, either the rising and falling of your abdomen or the air flowing through the tip of your nose. Stay for a period of at least fifteen minutes or as long as you wish.

Keep focussing on the muscle in the solar plexus, on the rising and falling or on your nostrils at the tip of your nose as the air goes by. You can feel the air passing with the in breath, and the out breath.

Swami Ramdass, a devout Indian saint, explains:

"You are like a gatekeeper. Your job is to focus your awareness on your primary object of the breath in the gentlest way possible. Your awareness is going to wander; it is going to be grabbed by many stray thoughts. When you detect these, just return to watching the breath; gently bringing your mind back to your awareness. Don't try to push your thoughts away violently. Just be the observer. They're just thoughts. Very gently, again and again, simply bring your awareness back to the primary object of meditation: breathing in, breathing out. Just keep com-

ing back to the focus of your meditation, back to the breath, back to awareness of the breath."

Notice that you are only an observer, whether your breathing is fast or slow; just observe, allow it to be the way it is. Do not try to change it. You are aware and you are working in yourself. You are the gatekeeper simply watching the gate open and close, and your breath. Accept and observe any sounds, smells, or sensations around and let them all go. Always bringing your awareness back to either the rising and falling or breathing in and breathing out.

If your mind wanders into the past, into the future or any thoughts, just notice it. Then with gentleness bring it back to breathing in and breathing out. Wherever your mind is, just observe and notice where it is. If it helps you can repeat internally to yourself, "breathing in, breathing out" with each breath. If you like to count your breath, try counting to ten, coordinating with each in and out breath cycle. If your mind wanders, observe it, you can keep your inner smile and start over. Sometimes it can be hard to concentrate, but try not judge yourself, you do not need frustration; there is no success or failure, only your awareness, only the practice of breathing in peace for yourself and the whole planet.

When we practice this kind of meditation there is nothing we need to think about other than observing the breathing in and breathing out or rising and falling. Notice this life force within you, and the shape and form as the breath goes by—the start, middle, and end of each breath; the space in between; the beginning, middle, and end of the in and out breath; and again the space.

Even if anxiety arises, or boredom or bliss or anything, just observe. See it as another thought. Notice it, keep witnessing. It is only you and your observation. Bring your awareness back to rising and falling or breathing in and breathing out. Allow your breath to help you by taking a few deep intentional breaths. And observe all the feelings in your body, all sensations, tastes, smells, sounds, sights, just notice their existence and impermanence, how they come and go, and then bring your awareness back to the breath.

Make sure you sit firm with your head straight in alignment with your spine, release your shoulders and open your chest. Feel the freedom and peace the meditation can bring to your mind. Observe the last minutes of your sitting meditation using it consciously.

"There is no beginning and no end. Every breath is the first and last."—said Ramdass. The Indian saint continued: *"Gently but firmly bring your mind back each time it wanders. Be vigilant but gentle. Bring the awareness back to the basic primary object of meditation: basic attention to the breath. If your mind becomes agitated throughout the course of the day bring it back to the breath. Breathing in and breathing out. Your breath is your anchor. And it is the most beautiful and precious gift you can have. Be aware of it."*

Walking Meditation

The art of walking meditation has long been one of my favorite practices. During walking meditation we recognize the miracle in simply walking, the unification of the body and mind. It helps one deal with difficult emotions such as anger, anxiety, and more. Inspired by the beloved Zen master Thich Nhat Hanh and his experience with mindfulness over 55 years, I have long been practicing walking meditation with so much joy.

The text below is an extract of an article by Thich Nhat Hanh, from *Lion's Roar*, on May 31, 2019. With their permission, I reproduce the article to give you a taste of walking meditation's beauty.

"The practice of mindful walking is a profound and pleasurable way to deepen our connection with our body and the earth. We breathe, take a mindful step, and come back to our true home.

Many of us walk for the sole purpose of getting from one place to another. Now suppose we are walking to a sacred place. We would walk quietly and take each gentle step with reverence. I propose that we walk this way every time we walk on the earth. The earth is sacred and we touch her with each step. We should be very respectful, because we are walking on our mother. If we walk like that, then every step will be grounding, every step will be nourishing.

We can train ourselves to walk with reverence. Wherever we walk, whether it's the railway station or the supermarket, we are walking on the earth and so we are in a holy sanctuary. If we remember to walk like that, we can be nourished and find solidity with each step.

To walk in this way, we have to notice each step. Each step made in mindfulness can bring us back to the here and the now. Go slowly. Mindfulness lights our way. We don't rush. With each breath we may take just one step. We may have run all our life, but now we don't have to run anymore. This is the time to stop running. To be grounded in the earth is to feel its solidity with each step and know that we are right where we are supposed to be.

Each mindful breath, each mindful step, reminds us that we are alive on this beautiful planet. We don't need anything else. It is wonderful enough just to be alive, to breathe in, and to make one step. We have arrived at where real life is available—the present moment. If we breathe and walk in this way, we become as solid as a mountain.

There are those of us who have a comfortable house, but we don't feel that we are home. We don't want anything, and yet we don't feel home. All of us are looking for our solid ground, our true home. The earth is our true home and it is always there, beneath us and around us. Breathe, take a mindful step, and arrive. We are already at home.

Uniting Body and Mind

We can't be grounded in our body if our mind is somewhere else. We each have a body that has been given us by the earth. This body is a wonder. In our daily lives, we may spend many hours forgetting the body. We get lost in our computer or in our worries, fear, or busyness. Walking meditation makes us whole again. Only when we are connected with our body are we truly alive. Healing is not possible without that connection. So walk and breathe in such a way that you can connect with your body deeply.

Walking meditation unites our body and our mind. We combine our breathing with our steps. When we breathe in, we may take two or three steps. When we breathe out, we may take three, four, or five steps. We pay attention to what is comfortable for our body.

Our breathing has the function of helping our body and mind to calm down. As we walk, we can say, *Breathing in, I calm my body, Breathing out, I bring peace into my body.* Calming the breath calms the body and reduces any pain and tension.

Walking meditation is first and foremost a practice to bring body and mind together peacefully.

When we walk like this, with our breath, we bring our body and our mind back together. Our body and our mind are two aspects of the same reality. If we remove our mind from our body, our body is dead. If we take our body out of our mind, our mind is dead. Don't think that one can be if the other is not.

No matter what we do, the place to start is to calm down, because when our mind and our body have calmed down, we see more clearly. When we see our anger or sadness clearly, it dissipates. We begin to feel more compassion for ourselves and others. We can only feel this when body and mind are united.

Walking meditation should not be work. It is very pleasant, especially in the early morning when the air is still very fresh. When we walk mindfully, we see the beauty and the wonder of the earth around us, and we wake up. We see that we are living a very wonderful moment. If our mind is caught and preoccupied with our worries and suffering, we miss these things. We can value each step we take, and each step brings us happiness. When we look again at the earth and the sky, we see that the earth is a wonderful reality.

We Are Not Separate From the Earth

We think that the earth is the earth and we are something outside of the earth. But in fact we are inside of the earth. Imagine that the earth is the tree and we are a leaf. The earth is not the environment, something outside of us that we need to care for. The earth is us. Just as your parents, ancestors, and teachers are inside you, the earth is in you. Taking care of the earth, we take care of ourselves.

When we see that the earth is not just the environment, that the earth is in us, at that moment you can have real communion with the earth. But if we see the earth as only the environment, with ourselves in the center, then we only want to do something for the earth in order for us to survive. But it is not enough to take care of the earth. That is a dualistic way of seeing.

We have to practice looking at our planet not just as matter, but as a living and sentient being. The universe, the sun, and the stars have contributed many elements to the earth, and when we look into the earth we see that it's a very beautiful flower containing the presence of the whole universe. When we look into our own bodily formation, we are made of the same elements as the planet. It has made us. The earth and the universe are inside of us.

When we take mindful steps on the earth, our body and mind unite, and we unite with the earth. The earth gave birth to us and the earth will receive us again. Nothing is lost. Nothing is born. Nothing dies. We don't need to wait until after our body has disintegrated to go back to Mother Earth. We are going back to Mother Earth at every moment. Whenever we breathe, whenever we step, we are returning to the earth. Even when we scratch ourselves, skin cells will fall and return to the earth.

Breathing in, I know Mother Earth is in me.
Breathing out, I know Mother Earth is in me.

Earth includes the life sphere and the atmosphere. So you don't have to wait until you die to go back to Mother Earth, because you are already in Mother Earth. We have to return to take refuge in our beautiful planet. I know that earth is my home. I don't need to die in order to go back to Mother Earth. I am in Mother Earth right now, and Mother Earth is in me.

You may like to try this exercise while you walk: Breathing in, I know Mother Earth is in me. Breathing out, I know Mother Earth is in me.

Paul Tillich, the German theologian, said, "God is not a person but not less than a person." This is true of the earth as well. It is more than a person. It has given birth to millions of species, including human beings. Many ancient cultures believed there was a deity that inhabited the sun, and they worshiped the sun. But when I do walking meditation and touching the earth, I do not have that kind of dualistic view. I am not worshiping the earth as a separate deity outside of myself.

I think of the earth as a bodhisattva, a great and compassionate being. A bodhisattva is a being who has awakening, understanding, and love. Any living being who has awakening, peace, understanding, and love can be called a bodhisattva, but a bodhisattva doesn't have to be a human being. When we look into a tree, we see the tree is fresh, it nourishes life, and it offers shade and beauty. It's a place of refuge for so many birds and other creatures. A bodhisattva is not something that is up in the clouds far away from us. Bodhisattvas are all around us. A young person who has love, who has freshness, who has understanding, who offers us a lot of happiness, is a bodhisattva. The pine standing in the garden gives us joy, offers us oxygen, and makes life more beautiful.

When we say that earth is a beautiful bodhisattva, this is not our imagination. It is a fact that the earth is giving life and she is very beautiful. The bodhisattva is not a separate spirit inhabiting the earth; we should transcend that idea. There are not two separate things—the earth, which is a material thing, and the spirit of the earth, a nonmaterial thing that inhabits the earth.

Our planet earth is itself a true, great bodhisattva. It embodies so many great virtues. The earth is solid—it can carry so many things. It is patient—it takes its time moving glaciers and carving rocks. The earth doesn't discriminate. We can throw fragrant flowers on the earth, or we can throw urine and excrement on the earth, and the earth purifies it. The earth has a great capacity to endure, and it offers so much to nourish us—water, shelter, food, and air to breathe.

When we recognize the virtues, the talent, the beauty of the earth bodhisattva, love is born. You love the earth and the earth loves you. You would do anything for the well-being of the earth. And the earth will do anything for your well-being. That is the natural outcome of the real loving relationship. The earth is not just your environment, to be taken care of or worshiped; you are each other. Every mindful step can manifest that love.

With each step the earth heals us, and with each step we heal the earth.

Part of love is responsibility. In Buddhism, we speak of meditation as an act of awakening. To awaken is to be awake to something. We need to be awake to the fact that the earth is in danger and living species on earth are also in danger. When we walk mindfully, each step reminds us of our responsibility. We have to protect the earth with the same commitment we have to protect our family and ourselves. The earth can nourish and heal us but it suffers as well. With each step the earth heals us, and with each step we heal the earth.

When we walk mindfully on the face of the earth, we are grounded in her generosity and we cannot help but be grateful. All of the earth's qualities of patience, stability, creativity, love, and non-discrimination are available to us when we walk reverently, aware of our connection.

Let the Buddha Walk

I have a student named Sister Tri Hai who spent a long time in prison. She was a peace activist I knew since she was in middle school. She came to the United States to study English literature before going back to Vietnam and becoming a nun. When she was out in the streets advocating for peaceful change, she was arrested and put in prison.

During the day, the prison guards didn't like her to sit in meditation. When they see someone sitting in a prison cell solidly and stably, it feels a bit threatening. So she waited until the lights had gone out, and she would sit like a person who has freedom. In outer appearance she was caught in the prison. But inside she was completely free. When you sit like that, the walls are not there. You're in touch with the whole universe. You have more freedom than people outside who are imprisoning themselves in their agitation.

Sister Tri Hai also practiced walking meditation in her prison cell. It was very small — after seven steps she had to turn around and come back. Sitting and walking mindfully gave her space inside. She taught other prisoners in her cell how to sit and how to breathe so they would suffer less. They were in a cold cell, but through their walking meditation, they were grounded in the solid beauty of the earth.

Those of us who can walk on the earth, who can walk in freedom, should do it. If we rush from one place to another, without practicing walking meditation, it is such a waste. What is walking for? Walking is for nothing. It's just for walking. That is our ultimate aim — walking in the spring breeze. We have to walk so that we have happiness, so that we can be a free person. We have to let go of everything, and not seek or long or search for anything. There is enough for us to be happy.

All the Buddhist stories tell us that the Buddha had a lot of happiness when he sat, when he walked, when he ate. We have some experience of this. We know there are moments when we're walking or sitting that we are so happy. We also know that there are times, because of illness or physical disability or because our mind is caught elsewhere, when we cannot walk freely like the Buddha. There are those of us who do not have the use of our legs. There are those of us who are in prison, like Sister Tri Hai, and only have a few feet of space. But we can all invite the Buddha to walk for us. When we have difficulty, we can leave that difficulty behind and let the Buddha walk for us. In a while the solidity of the earth can help us return to ourselves.

If we sit mindfully, if we walk mindfully and reverently on the earth, we will generate the energies of mindfulness, of peace, and of compassion in both body and mind.

We are made of body and mind. Our body can radiate the energy of peace and compassion. Our mind also has energy. The energy of the mind can be powerful. If the energy of the mind is filled with fear and anger, it can be very destructive. But if we sit mindfully, if we walk mindfully and reverently on the earth, we will generate the energies of mindfulness, of peace, and of compassion in both body and mind. This kind of energy can heal and transform.

If you walk reverently on the earth with two other people, soaking in the earth's solidity, you will all three radiate and benefit from the energy of peace and compassion. If three hundred people sit or walk like this, each one generates the energy of mindfulness, peace, and compassion, and everyone in the group receives that healing energy. The energy of peace and mindfulness does not come from elsewhere. It comes from us. It comes from our capacity to breathe, to walk, to sit mindfully and recognize the wonders of life.

When you walk reverently and solidly on this earth and I do the same, we send out waves of compassion and peace. It is this compassion that will heal ourselves, each other, and this beautiful green earth.

Meditation: Walking on the Earth

Walk slowly, in a relaxed way. When you practice this way, your steps are those of the most secure person on earth. Feel the gravity that makes every step attach to the earth. With each step, you are grounded on the earth.

One way to practice walking meditation is to breathe in and take one step, and focus all your attention on the sole of your foot. If you have not arrived fully, 100 percent in the here and the now, don't take the next step. I'm sure you can take a step like that because there is Buddha Nature in you. Buddha Nature is the capacity of being aware of what is going on. It is what allows you to recognize what you are doing in the current moment and to say to yourself, I am alive, I am taking a step. Anyone can do this. There is a Buddha in every one of us, and we should allow the Buddha to walk.

While walking, practice conscious breathing by counting steps. Notice each breath and the number of steps you take as you breathe in and as you breathe out. Don't try to control your breathing. Allow your lungs as much time and air as they need, and simply notice how many steps you take as your lungs fill up and how many you take as they empty, mindful of both your breath and your steps. The link is the counting.

When you walk uphill or downhill, the number of steps per breath will change. Always follow the needs of your lungs. You may notice that your exhalation is longer than your inhalation. You might find that you take three steps during your in-breath and four steps during your out-breath, or two steps, then three steps. If this is comfortable for you, please enjoy practicing this way. You can also try making the in-breath and the out-breath the same length, so that you take three steps with your in-breath and three with your out-breath. Keep walking and you will find the natural connection between your breath and your steps.

Don't forget to practice smiling. Your half-smile will bring calm and delight to your steps and your breath, and help sustain your attention. After practicing for half an hour or an hour, you will find that your breath, your steps, your counting, and your half-smile all blend together in a marvellous balance of mindfulness. Each step grounds us in the solidity of the earth. With each step we fully arrive in the present moment.

Walking Meditation Poem

"I take refuge in Mother Earth.
Manifests our love.
Every breath brings happiness.
Every step brings happiness.
I see the whole cosmos in the earth."

THE POWER OF VISUALIZATION

In short, visualization is about creating all the pictures in your mind of the things you want to achieve and experience in life. Visualization is usually paired with meditation and mindfulness. What this process would look like is going to a quiet place, closing your eyes and calming your body, and starting to think about the things you want to experience in life. During this process, you want to get as detailed as you possibly can.

To add this practice into your life you just need to find a quiet place to sit or lie down. Make sure this is a place where you will not be disturbed. Close your eyes and take several deep breaths to help yourself relax. Begin to think about the outcome, object, or situation that you want in your life. Think about it as clearly as possible with every detail that you can imagine. Make sure that you add into your visualization your feelings and emotions related to what you are visualizing.

Practice doing this at least once a day, but preferably more. You don't have to spend hours visualizing. It can be something that you do for just five or ten minutes every time you get started. When you have finished visualizing, it's important that you continue to maintain a good attitude about whatever it is that you are visualizing. It's not going to help you visualize if you spend the rest of the day thinking that what you're visualizing is impossible. Instead, continue to hold on to the belief that you can achieve in your life, believe in your potential.

If you're new to the idea of visualization, you may find yourself questioning if it can actually work and how. Visualization is simply training your mind. In a way, you are practicing for experiencing whatever it is that you want to experience and achieve in your life.

The more you focus on something, the more likely you are to see it happening. The more you visualize it, the more you are able to really see and believe in it. You will look for the opportunities to make it happen and the universe will respond to you accordingly. Remember: what you give to life is what life gives to you.

The actual science behind visualization relates to the neural patterns of your brain. As you continue to think and visualize the things that you want in your life, you create neural patterns, the same way as if you had actually done that activity. This is why basketball players are able to increase the percentage of shots they make. They train their brain for how to succeed at shooting by visualizing it. The nervous system of your body is stimulated just by thinking about something, even if you have never taken part in the activity before.

Whenever we perceive a manifestation with our physical senses, we're actually perceiving the projection of its nonphysical form, which is created by the mental energies through intense focus, belief and feeling. A large percentage of the manifestation process is already completed by the time you begin to translate it into physical experience. In other words, the vibration of the thing you imagined was already real even before you could detect it.

Time is irrelevant in a universe that is pure energy. You're merely spending what is considered time by adjusting your frequency to match this new reality. What is more, building upon it with focus will make your physical senses able to detect it. So your mind and emotional states do the real creating for you. You are then able to perceive these things with the faculties of your physical senses, and your frequency will match the frequency of the desired manifestation. You can sense its energy with your mind and imagination. At that moment, you are tuning into the frequency of it in a nonphysical form.

Even if you are not able to see it in your mind, you can perceive it. All it takes is having the imagination to create it. As you visualize, feel the emotion of it. Once again, by allowing yourself to visualize in a state of total relaxation and detachment, you should be able to sense immediately how it feels to have this manifestation in your presence. Absorb yourself in those feeling states and sit with them as long as you wish, or until they are no longer heightened.

Although your physical senses are able to receive these changes immediately, when you understand that you are readjusting your frequency and building the frequency you desire, it makes the process seem much more logical and easier to understand. Your physical senses are only able to pick up slight energetic shifts in the direction of your dreams as your senses adjust themselves to perceive the frequencies you created. Your visualization has immediately been created in the nonphysical, but in order for you to see it in physical form, you must turn yourself toward its direction.

What everyone really wants, the thing behind their dreams and desires, is the nonphysical frequency range. It's the emotions and the feelings that we are all reaching for. For example, prosperity, abundance, generosity and beautiful relationships are simply projections of the nonphysical manifestations. The underlying meaning behind each of these things is how they make us feel. We don't actually desire the physical manifestation—we desire the feeling state. This is why trying to manifest the physical form of what we dream or desire creates a weak intention. But most importantly, you must surrender, let go, and detach yourself from control. We must trust this supreme intelligence and how the universe operates.

It's not the physical manifestation that ultimately satisfies us, it's the feeling state. Focusing on the physical manifestation rather than the feeling you truly want from it is like trying to satisfy your appetite with a picture of something you would like to eat rather than having the food itself. Put all your creative energy into manifesting your nonphysical dreams and desires, because that is what you truly want. The deeper meaning is carried by the energetic aspect of the frequencies, or how you feel when you think about already having it. Through our feelings, we begin to align our frequency with our dreams, therefore manifesting and bringing them into our experience.

Always set your intention in your heart and allow the projection of that to come to you. Eventually, your frequency and the frequency of your dream will match. Your physical senses will catch up with it, and you will see your dreams manifesting in physical form. Through the vibrations of the heart and brain we send out a frequency, reaching out and connecting with others who are on the same frequency. At the frequencies of love and acceptance, you reach trust and surrender, and fear can no longer control you. Tune yourself into love and you will see the energy flow and guide you.

Learn What You Really Want

Visualization has the power to improve performance, deliver better results, and boost your productivity. You're training your mind to focus through the visualization process. You are getting into the routine of calming your mind, training yourself to focus on one thing at a time. When you spend time visualizing, you get in tune with yourself, and understand yourself better. You're able to see the things you want to achieve and experience in life. This helps you to understand on a deeper level why you want those things. Working through visualizations helps you to come up with clear goals and really understand what it is that you want.

When you take time to visualize, you're taking time out of your day, and that helps you to get away from the stress in your life. You are calming yourself from the inside out, which can help alleviate stress. You are learning how to control your thoughts. This is an important ability to have if you are constantly living in stressful situations. Visualization allows you to take control of what you are thinking about and how your body is reacting.

By continuing to practice visualization, you can learn to control your body's reaction and calm your mind even in the midst of a difficult situation when you don't have time to step away and find a quiet place. These practices can also be used when you are trying to fall asleep.

There are very many successful people that practice it. Tony Robbins has been teaching visualization for many years. According to him, "Whatever you hold in your mind on a consistent basis is exactly what you will experience in your life."

Maximize your Visualization

To tap into the power of visualization, focus your mind like a laser and see what happens when you invoke this power within yourself. As you do this, be aware of the beautiful way this power is being used for good and how it creates a better version of yourself. Use it for your highest good because happiness and freedom are your birth right.

Try it yourself, using the power of imagination and visualization. First, take a few breaths in awareness. Maybe three deep breaths to start, or as many as you need to fully connect with this present moment. Then visualize our beautiful blue planet, Mother Earth, in all its beauty. Visualize our galaxy, the Milky Way, existing among infinite other galaxies. This is our reality and the cosmic dream we live in.

Now visualize, with a stronger power, that you are sending everything that does not serve you back to the Universe, as if there was a big cosmic recycling bin. You can even picture a bright shooting light going away from you, sending back to the Universe all of your pain and suffering. In this way, you send away all your doubts, pains, and sufferings from your past or present. Why should you keep all this negativity for yourself? Doubts create heavy viruses in the system, which stop you from experiencing your full potential. Replace them with trust, and trust the Universe. At the same time, name the emotions and beliefs that are blocking you and send them back to the Universe, letting it take care of the negative emotions for you.

Once you have sent them all away, the space will be open for positivity and light. This space should not be left empty: fill it with whatever is it you want to experience. Put into words exactly what you want to attract, what dreams your soul is yearning to experience. Visualize them coming from the universe, with a bright, shining light, as you fill this space with this newfound love.

There is no point living a life without smiles, laughs, love, and joy. If we cannot laugh and smile, then we are wasting precious time.

We are here to be happy and to experience the ultimate freedom. Life is short and we should live out all our dreams before we die. We lose time with ideas of suffering, accepting our circumstances instead of opening our wings in search for more. It is not you as an individual who causes all your suffering, but your mental programming. When we clean our minds, then we are able to live our dreams.

With visualization, you can remove old blockages from your system and install new programs.

Cleansing your system is not a one-time occurrence. You can do this process every time you feel it is necessary. Keep in mind that to bring forth a new experience, you need to clearly state what it is you want to experience. The clearer you are with your visualization, the easier it will manifest. The more you understand the process and what you are feeling, the more you will be able to clean out all those negative feelings and past memories that have been kept inside.

I am repeating myself to make sure you get it! Take out all your garbage with the power of visualization. There is an infinite source of power in the universe available for us; we just need to learn how to access it. The Universe is always responding to us, so make sure you put consciousness in every word, action, and thought.

Visualization is actually very simple. Indeed, it is one of the most powerful techniques for resetting the operating system we are running. It is so simple that it is hard to believe. Most of the time, people like to complicate things, but activating this power inside of us will help clean up any energetic blockages we are experiencing.

If you want to step out of the karmic wheel, you need to learn to trust the Universe. Remember: it is your birth right to be happy and free. We should not force any truth onto anyone. If your heart feels the truth, then listen to it. Trust it. All in all, we cannot force anything onto somebody who is not ready to receive it. But by trusting the Universe, everything will come at the right time and place.

You are the most powerful and beautiful being you could ever imagine. You are amazing, but your doubts are stopping you from realizing and experiencing who you truly are. Doubts are mental pollution that belong in the cosmic recycling bin. Do not allow doubt to enter your system, because your true essence is pure love! Keep cleaning up your system and tuning your mind, and you will finally find the gold and diamonds that are buried in your heart. They will appear, and you will start to shine again, and you will understand how precious you are.

Connecting with Our Beloveds

Now, I will teach you another very simple visualization technique that allows you to connect with anyone you wish. The power of infinite intelligence is beyond rationality and comprehension.

Make sure you are relaxed and will not be disturbed or interrupted. Just close your eyes, breathe, and envisage the person you wish to connect with. Alive or dead, it does not matter. Just imagine this person arriving at the place you wish to meet, and then start a conversation with him or her. Ask questions and listen carefully to what they have to tell you. For example, you could ask for advice and guidance.

This meditation technique can give us amazing insights. Most of all, it helps us connect with the infinite source of intelligence that lies within us all. When I first did it at my sister's home in Brazil, it was a super crazy quick experience. I was relaxing on the sofa, no one was home; as I put on a soundtrack, I started the visualization. I imagined that I was talking to Anandamurti[4], such a beloved master whom I never had the chance to meet when he was alive, but I deeply loved through his teachings and disciples. I invited Anandamurti to sit next to me near the fire in my home in Switzerland. I said I was honored that he had come, and in a very casual way, I asked if he had some suggestions for me, anything that could help me at that moment. I wanted something to support my spiritual journey. Very clearly he answered, "Look for the next retreat. It is very near you." I got my answer. Okay. I understood. I thanked him. And that was it. Half awake, half sleep, my visualization did not take more than a few minutes.

It was really quick and as I finished, I turned on my computer and checked for retreats in Europe. To my astonishment, I found out there would be a retreat in Switzerland, less than two hours by train from my home. It was to be a unique event gathering people from all over the world, which had last happened in that same place 40 years ago. I got goosebumps, and thought *Wow, this works!* Given

---

4 Prabhat Ranjan Sarkar (21 May 1921 – 21 October 1990) also known as Ánandamúrti or Bábá ("Father") to his disciples, was a spiritual guru, philosopher, poet and great composer. He founded Ananda Marga (the Path of Bliss) in 1955 as a spiritual and social organization that continues to offer instruction in meditation and yoga.

that I had not heard about this retreat before, how could I have imagined it, if not directly from my beloved master?

That same day, I received a message from a friend who also loves Anandamurti. I asked him if he knew about this retreat and he said yes. He asked me, “How did you know about it?” And I answered, “Anandamurti himself told me during my meditation.” We were both simply amazed. This is just one example of how things work when the mind is focused and open to receive. It is beautiful and magical to know that we can use the power of our minds, and at the same time get out of linear thinking and expand our potential.

When millions of people start creating this kind of focus in their minds, we will make positive changes for the earth and for our consciousness. With optimism and an open mind, we can start manifesting dreams into reality, but we must focus on *what we want.* Only then will magic unfold. A focused mind can penetrate the cosmos. Whenever we get an idea, if we make sure it comes from love, we will not be wasting time and energy. When you do it with love, eventually you will succeed in whatever you do. Love is the answer we have all been waiting for.

Yoga Subtle Science

Yoga is a spiritual discipline based on a very subtle science, which focuses on bringing harmony between mind and body. Yoga does not adhere to any particular religion, belief system or community; it has always been approached as a technology for inner well-being. It is the art and science of healthy living.

The word yoga is derived from the Sanskrit root Yuj, meaning to join or to yoke or to unite. As per yogic scriptures, the practice of yoga leads to the union of individual consciousness with that of the Universal Consciousness, indicating a perfect harmony between the mind and body, man & nature. According to modern science, everything in the universe is just a manifestation of the same quantum firmament. One who experiences this oneness of existence is said to be in yoga, and is termed as a yogi, having attained a state of freedom referred to as mukti, nirvana, or moksha. Thus the aim of yoga is self-realization; to overcome all kinds of suffering, leading to this state of liberation and freedom. Living with freedom in all walks of life, health, and harmony are the main objectives of yoga practice. Overall, yoga is about harmonizing oneself with the universe. It is the technology of aligning individual geometry with the cosmic, to achieve the highest level of perception and harmony.

Yoga also refers to an inner science comprising a variety of methods through which human beings can realize this union and achieve mastery over their destiny. Yoga, being widely considered as an immortal cultural outcome of Indus Saraswati Valley civilization—dating back to 2700 B.C.—has proved itself as catering to both the material and spiritual uplifting of humanity. Basic humane values are the very identity of yoga sadhana.

The *Yoga Sutra*, a 2,000-year-old treatise on yogic philosophy by the Indian sage Patanjali, is a guidebook on how to master the mind, control the emotions, and grow spiritually. The *Yoga Sutr*a is the earliest written record of yoga and one of the oldest texts in existence and provides the framework for all modern yoga. Various styles of yoga combine physical postures, breathing techniques, and meditation or relaxation. In more recent years, it has become popular as a form of physical exercise based upon poses that promote improved control of the mind and body and enhance well-being. Yoga is well known for its postures and poses, but this is only a small fraction of original yoga traditions in India. Fitness is not a primary goal. Practitioners and followers of yogic tradition focus instead on other practices, such as expanding spiritual energy using breathing methods and mental focus.

Most people in the West, and also many in India, confuse yoga with hatha yoga, the system of bodily postures. But yoga is primarily a spiritual discipline. The body is a part of our human nature, and must be kept fit so it doesn't obstruct our spiritual efforts. However, it is not the main focus of self-realization.

For many, the practice of yoga is restricted to hatha yoga and asanas (postures). However, among the yoga sutras, just three sutras are dedicated to asanas. Fundamentally, hatha yoga is a preparatory process so that the body can sustain higher levels of energy. The process begins with the body, then the breath, the mind, and the inner self.

Indeed, yoga is a wonderful practice that unifies the body, mind and soul. Every day, we have 24 new hours full of possibilities and opportunities. It is possible to create more flexibility in our bodies and ourselves. For many of us, the body and the mind have become rigid, and the energy is not flowing freely. Not only has our body lost its flexibility, but so has our mind. When the mind is not open to new ideas, it is unable to change its current paradigms and detach from social beliefs. This creates stagnant energy that prevents creativity, connection, and nourishment within and between one another.

On the physical level, hatha yoga relates to the articulations of the body. By turning the body from one side to the other, you might release any blocked energies. We can turn upside down, move from side to side, squat, roll, or do anything that moves our spine in order to let the energy circulate in our bodies. We can stretch up to the sky and all the way back down to Earth. When you stretch your body regularly, you can feel the effects in your whole being, as the mind and spirit are also opening.

Yoga postures or asanas do have a positive effect on the body, mind, further helping us to open up. The objective is to calm the mind and body, preparing it for meditation and awakening and activating this energy within. As you go deeper into each pose, you also stretch your mind. What does it mean to stretch the mind? It means to reach a little further, to open up to new ideas, possibilities, ways of thinking, challenges and experiences.

As we grow older, some of us might become attached to our own personality, to memories we've accumulated and the illusions of our identity—things that are not our true essence. We think we are our ideas and judgments, but that is not the case. Why should we become harder and more rigid with the passing years?

We are born to be free, to appreciate the wonders of life and of our own nature and divine being, and to experience love and compassion. It is when you let go of everything you think you are—your nationality, culture, belief systems, etc.—that you stretch your body, existence, and mind, and reach your true being. Our body, mind and spirit are connected on a deeper level, and when one is out of balance, the whole system is affected. Yoga can help us get back to that balance, bringing awareness of the body, mind, and spirit. All of it is interconnected.

Yoga cannot be separated from meditation. When practicing yoga, make sure you combine it with meditation, or else it will become merely a form of physical exercise. Although that is a good starting point, it is far from the true meaning of yoga. If the kind of yoga you have been practicing does not include a meditation practice, you can do research on isha yoga, kundalini yoga, Ananda Marga, Self-realization Fellowship, sahaja yoga and many other kinds of integrative yoga.

Yoga invokes a very effective, therapeutic response that can be seen after just a few weeks of practice. Recently, a woman who was joining us for yoga and meditation told me that her husband felt as if he had a new wife. I was so happy to hear that she was feeling renewed life energy. This is why yoga is regarded around the world as an effective practice and therapy. It is natural, and it is not an activity limited to the mind or the body. It is, in fact, a lifestyle, and it contains a philosophy much deeper than what is commonly practiced in most Western yoga classes.

11. UBUNTU SEEDS

The biggest happiness comes when we can delight together. There is a word for this: *Ubuntu*. This state was discovered by an anthropologist while he was studying the social behaviors of an African tribe. The meaning has no direct translation in English, but it summarizes the feeling of experiencing happiness as a tribe rather than as an individual. The anthropologist studied the behavior of children within an African tribe and conducted several social experiments. One of these experiments tested how children reacted during a competition. He placed a basket of fresh fruit underneath a tree and explained to them that whoever reached the basket first could take the delicious fruits home as a prize. He drew a starting line in the dirt and started to count down.

Most children and adults in Western culture are programmed to be competitive when faced with a physical challenge such as this. What we typically witness from children in such a scenario is the hunger for victory, the desire to showcase some form of superiority. This competitiveness seems to be ingrained in our mental programming, or even in our DNA, but what the anthropologist observed shocked him.

On "GO", the children remained stationary for a moment, then linked their arms, holding hands, smiling, and skipped in unison over to the fruit basket. Each one took a seat around the tree, and they all enjoyed the fruits as a group. The spontaneous and authentic decision they made together produced no losers, only winners. They had supported each other along the way to make it to the finish line, so they could all enjoy the reward together.

The researcher, puzzled yet moved by the display, asked them why they acted in such a way. They explained it was "Ubuntu", which means: "I am because you are." It is oneness. An individual cannot fully embrace joy if other members of their society are in emotional or physical pain. In their view, they are all one. This is Ubuntu.

Competition brings us challenges and stress, and it does not bring us true happiness. Some people believe they are winners, and some believe they are losers, but we are really winning when we share happiness and blessings. We need to let go of all ideas and concepts that do not serve us on our quest for peace and happiness, and at the same time break down unfavorable systems in our mind. Positive vibrations can shift consciousness, allowing us to elevate our understanding. Understanding deeply from within becomes "innerstanding."

It was only because the children joined hands and ran as one group that they were all able to reach the basket and share the fruits together. In the same way, we can join our hands and support and share this love and happiness. It might seem like a fantasy, in a world where war is still very prevalent, but I am a dreamer, and this is a time for revolution and expansion. The healing seeds of Ubuntu can then spread in all directions.

Remember that we are all free, but it is our choice. We have one inner world and we can create and experience hell or heaven inside ourselves. Look in the mirror and smile. Say to yourself "*I love you.*" No matter what, remember that you have the power. You can smile at life and choose to see the beauty of it. Your smile will empower you even more, and it will help you create more positive changes. It is all a big cosmic joke anyway, and it is pure magic.

When I was hang-gliding or paragliding, I could feel the energy of Ubuntu inside me. I was not just experiencing it externally but felt it deep inside. I was taking the opportunity of flying to internally expand myself. I also remember feeling frustration, seeing so many pilots having the same opportunity but not using it to open their minds and hearts. Many of them were only using it to reinforce their egos and sense of control and power. From that time on, it was clear that all I wanted was to become a better person and develop more wisdom. Flying or not, that was not the point. I understood that there were many ways to experience different dimensions of reality, and in the following years, I would learn how to fly from within using different meditation techniques. I no longer needed to physically go anywhere to obtain this, I just had to dream.

Ubuntu is a new way of understanding. It is a way for us as humans to be more helpful to each other and to reach heaven on Earth. We can come together as a family and appreciate all that Mother Earth provides. We do not need to compete, this is not the natural way of the heart. Adopting Ubuntu as our primary philosophy will make our soul feel a great deal richer. Let us join hands and be together on this journey, so that we may nourish ourselves and others around us. It is time for spiritual evolution and revolution!

Are you ready for transformation? Are you willing to expand your potential? To discover the essence of true beauty within? Will you allow it to manifest from the metaphysical to experience it as true reality?

We are here to awaken from our illusion of separateness.
Martin Luther King Jr

12. COSMIC REVOLUTIONARIES

This is a time of change and transformation; a planetary shift is already happening. We do not know how long it will take, but we can all feel it. Transformation is a time to purify our suffering. Through our suffering, the soul experiences darkness, and the light can finally enter. The dark night of the soul is not our enemy, but just a sense of non-light. Without the darkness, how would we know what light is?

Our imaginary enemies, such as fear and hate, are present only when the light within us is dim. It is our responsibility to reflect the light back into life. We awaken and protect this light within us by grounding our actions and decisions in love. This mindfulness is the most precious treasure of the heart. With it, the intensity of the light becomes stronger every day and we are able to see things with clarity.

I don't know how many years it will take the cosmic revolutionaries to bring this revolution to Earth, but if one individual can have such a strong influence, imagine what an entire awakened collective could generate when living in a state of love. We can learn to increase this power and intense light within ourselves as we become more conscious of it. There are many ways of increasing the intensity of our energy field and to keep it shining and expanding. With determination, we can keep moving in this direction, increasing the light within us. It is both an individual and collective matter. If we stay focused, we can reverse any negative condition in our life and planet. All we need is strong determination, knowing that we can reach a goal and that the Universe is with us, always supporting and helping us. Only when we become conscious of life's sacredness—and of what we want—can we help our planet and our future generations.

We are more than just humans, more than the illusion of the ego limiting us and our visions. We have a body that is alive and an intelligent mind to use. This mind can be very tricky if we do not understand it properly, but we can learn how to operate it for the sake of our own happiness. If we corrupt ourselves, we will end up getting sick and dying without having created a beautiful life story. We all know we will die sooner or later, that time will reveal age and death, but only when we operate through love can we transform for the better, just like many beautiful souls, cosmic revolutionaries and masters who have passed away and left their legacy, their dreams and their love in this physical world. Hence, it can be said that they are still living within us.

Masters of love never truly die; they became immortal and are still here with us. We are here together, on this spaceship, in this inner dream called Earth. Our beloved Mother Earth gives us new opportunities to see her beauty each and every day. We are cosmic revolutionaries! We are the rainbow people of all colors, made up of all different beautiful cosmic cells. Through our optic nerves, we can see all the magnificent colors and beauty of nature. We are part of a new generation, and we are getting ready for a big shift of consciousness and vibration on our planet. We are not here to sit around and wait but need action and the right attitude to do what is correct. We are movement, sound, and vibration. Along the way, we learn to tune ourselves to the Universe, so we can harmonize and expand with it. It's not enough to just talk or read about it, it's about taking action and transforming ourselves, healing ourselves, and healing Mother Earth. Life is about sharing! Share your love, share your heart, share your story. Share this story! Share everything as much as you can!

13.

THE MAGIC OF THE UNIVERSE

For over 20 years, I have been observing how the Universe loves each and every one of us, and I can tell you from my own experience: let your heart guide you, and do only what you love. Go in the direction of what you love, and make all your decisions based on love. See how everything just flows and how magic manifests when you lead a life in this manner. For that, the secret is love. God is love. Forget about the words, concepts, or ideas; just connect to the love that is inside of you. There are many ways to love. Life is always giving us signs to call us back to our true selves, which is our original state. If we listen to those calls, we can end suffering and enter the path of love.

I was calling the Universe, asking for help to become a better person, to be able to help others and do something beautiful with my life. To create a beautiful story that one day I could tell my children, to somehow help our generation and future generations. This was what I was asking for, and this is exactly what the Universe gave me.

Yes, once upon a time I was someone inside of a rainbow near the Himalayas, but that was just the beginning. This story of mine is a symbol, like everything else. The most important thing is your inner garden and spreading those seeds. Remember, your heart is your gift. Let's activate this energy of the heart and the divine force within to change, transform, and create new earth energy. Life is a beautiful dream if you choose to make it so.

I share this story out of pure love. Let's see what happens from the power of love, the power of the rainbow in action, manifested. This book was made out of this love and is written so all beloved ones might keep shining and passing the light on. This has been an exciting process of creativity. Seeds of gratitude are growing inside of me every day. I thank this divine energy, and I thank you.

CONTINUATION

The same way we cultivate our garden, we create our destiny. By observing nature deeply, we know that everything we plant grows. It is the very basic law of nature.

When I was writing this book, I had only a vague idea of how it would end. In the dream I saw our departure from Switzerland to go sailing around the world, ready for the adventure of living and crossing the oceans. It was just one of many dreams of mine. In this book, I have talked about the power of visualization and dreams, but still I am always surprised and enchanted by their magic.

After dreaming of our ocean life for almost 20 years, we finally made it happen. It was the opportunity to go wild again, away from the system, to create deep connections with nature and between our family, to discover the underwater life. To be with the dolphins, the whales and the stars, visiting amazing places on our planet.

We found an old catamaran on the border of Thailand and Malaysia—this was another crazy magical story I will tell you more about in the near future. In short, we repaired it and organized our departure from Switzerland. Then the Covid-19 pandemic hit and all borders closed. At the time of writing, we have still been unable to get back to the boat. But the catamaran and the dreams are waiting for us. After we left Switzerland, we went to a remote area in the south of Portugal, by the ocean, where I could finish this first book. Next, we are going to Brazil to visit our family, waiting for the borders to open and for our next adventure to start. I am curious about this next chapter of life and I will be happy to share this experience of living the dream with you.

We dream of sharing and inspiring others to set themselves free, and to create the conditions for their inner freedom and liberation—our final destination. This is possible, we can allow ourselves to dream, and live our dreams. We are all gardeners. Life is already a dream, we are all inside of it. We are the dream and the dreamers at the same time.

Some would ask, "Mukti, how can you manifest magic?" There is no scientific answer to this question, but I can affirm to you, it is all about trust, surrender, gratitude, and cultivating good seeds inside of ourselves. We dream with no attachments. We let go. We surrender to this infinite power and intelligence. We keep nurturing gratitude for everything that comes our way; it is the key for opening all doors. I just want to say thank you for all your love and for letting me share these seeds with you and for spreading these seeds all around you!

This is the birth of book one. But before this book came to life, it felt as if I was pregnant... the funny thing is that I found out it was twins! It became clear to me that I had two books coming out in this pregnancy. It was unexpected, it sounded funny and strange, but it was true. The two are very different, like dizygotic twins, fraternal or non-identical.

Book one is like a resume of my experiences united within some theoretical frame, in a very simple and spontaneous way. But book two is more of a sharing of my experiences that brought me to who I am today; personal stories entering my private life and adventures. Both books reflect the two twins, like the two hemispheres of our brain. The rational and analytical, the psychologist; and the other experiencing the art of living, the intuitive, dreamy one. It might be too much for Western minds. I don't know. I am just letting it be the way it is. And I am remembering to be grateful for everything. Book two is an intimate story of mine, in which I will tell you more about what happened with the rainbow. It is all part of my growth, inner evolution and insights. It is a story that for many may sound more like a fairy tale, but it is how I experience this awakened dream state called life. If you would like to let go of your rational mind and bring some magic into your life you might continue to book two.

The most important thing I want to tell you is that you are amazing; you too are a divine being. We all come from the same source and will return to the same source. And I hope I have been able to share my love with you, and that we can become better people together and help our beloved mother, brothers and sisters to love each other more, cultivating those beautiful seeds.

Breathing in and breathing out, just close your eyes, feel your heart. Feel your breath. Nourish love in each breath. Breathing in love. Breathing out gratitude.

If you liked this book, please, leave a review online, share and gift others. With your review and generosity you will make the difference and will be helping Mukti to share this message of love with many others around the world.

ABOUT THE AUTHOR

Born in Brazil, Mukti spent more than a decade studying Journalism and Psychology, and mastering Bio-psychology. Following her studies, she left for India and Nepal where she spent 11 years living in nature, practicing meditation and traveling. During this time, she worked as a spiritual tour guide, studied yoga and ayurveda. Mukti created her own virtual travel agency, taking groups into sacred spaces, monasteries, and holding retreats in the Himalayas. Along with from teaching Reiki, Mukti also became a paragliding tandem pilot, expressing her passion to fly and her free spirit.

While doing many expeditions into remote areas flying, living in the wild, bathing in the rivers and living in simple huts in nature; Mukti also wrote and produced the movie *Hanuman Airlines Fly over Everest*, together with Haminton Pevec, winning first prize in the St. Hilaire Festival, France, and the best public choice award. The film was also selected for the Banff Mountain Festival in Canada, where it was ranked among the 10 best movies of the year, and travelled to more than 40 countries.

At the same time, together with her Swiss husband and paragliding pioneer world acro champion, David Arrufat, Mukti created the non-profit International Association for Paragliding, APPI, helping pilots in more than 120 countries.

After more than two years of dedication to such a project, Mukti let go and left for the Philippines, deepening her meditation practices and living with her family in a raw food community, called Bahay Kalipay, next to its founder Pi Villaraza. It was here she got in contact with ancient Shamanism through the language of music and dreams.

In Brazil, Mukti had been inspired by Susan Andrews, and the Vision of the Future ecovillage, where she joined retreats in different eco-village prototypes involving permaculture, social work, ecology and spirituality. Later joining Maya's eco-village in the Philippines, Mukti then went on the create her own healing space in Switzerland, where she also founded the Swiss Mindfulness Institute, offering retreats and welcoming volunteers, teachers, healers and artists from all over the world.

Bringing it all together, Mukti keep planting and nourishing the seeds of love and compassion in her heart, and in the hearts of many. She believes that more and more eco-villages need to be created around the world, promoting sustainable and conscious living, and creating a new system of understanding and living on Earth.

Mukti, her husband David and their two children, Iara and Joy, are currently preparing to live onboard a catamaran in Thailand. She is creating film documentaries, while she writes the book that follows *Inside the Rainbow*, part of the *Rainbow Books* series. She continues to write about love, inspiring others and sharing more about rainbows, ancient wisdom, adventures and the beauty of life. Mukti's dream is to start The Ho'oponopono Village, an eco-village based on the principles of gratitude, love and forgiveness, manifesting and expressing dreams through music, art, yoga and ancient wisdom.

For more info and to receive Mukti's newsletter, including new release alerts, visit:
www.muktilove.com.

REFERENCES AND FURTHER READING

Shang C, "Emerging paradigms in mind-body medicine." *J Altern Complement Med*. 2001;

Tang Y.Y., Hölzel B.K., Posner M.I. "The neuroscience of mindfulness meditation." *Nature Reviews Neuroscience*. 2015;

Gerber R, *Vibrational Medicine*. Bear & Company; 1998.

Moss T, *Body Electric*. P. Tarcher; 1980.

Grossman P, "Mindfulness for psychologists: Paying kind attention to the perceptible." *Mindfulness*. 2010;

Thich Nhat Hanh *The Miracle of Mindfulness*. Parallax Press; 1975.

Buddharakkhita A. Metta, *The Philosophy and Practice of Universal Love*. Buddhist Publication Society; 1995.

Hopkins J, *Cultivating Compassion.* Broadway Books; 2001.

Analayo. Satipatthana, *The Direct Path to Realization*. Windhorse; 2003.

Cutler HC, *The Dalai Lama. The Art of Happiness: A Handbook for Living.* Riverhead Books; 1998.

The Dalai Lama. An Open Heart: Practicing compassion in everyday life. Little Brown and Company; 2001.

Sujiva V, *Loving-Kindness Meditation.* Buddha Dharma Education Association Inc; 1991.

Salzberg S, *Loving-Kindness.* Shambhala; 1995.

Sanharakshita, *Living with Kindness: The Buddha's Teaching on Metta.* Windhorse publications; 2004

Thich Nhat Hanh. *True Love: A Practice for Awakening the Heart.* Parallax Press; 1997.

Butler, Rhett. "Amazon Destruction." *Mongabay. com*, 23 Jan. 2016. Web. 25 July 2016.

Ingraham, Christopher. "How Beef Demand Is Accelerating the Amazon's Deforestation and Climate Peril." *Washington Post*. Web. 27 Aug. 2019.

Wisneski L, Anderson L, *The Scientific Basis of Integrative Medicine.* CRC Press; 2009;

Szent-Gyorgyi A, *Introduction to Submolecular Biology.* Academic Press; 1960.

Helmreic IS, “Potential energy and the body electric cardiac waves, brain waves, and the making of quantities into qualities.” *Curr Anthropol* 2013;

McCraty R, Atkinson M, Tomasino D, Bradley R. “The Coherent Heart: Heart-Brain Interactions, Psychophysiological Coherence, and the Emergence of System-Wide Order.” *Institute of HeartMath;* 2006.

Wakins A. *Mind–Body Medicine: A Clinician’s Guide to Psychoneuroimmunology.* Churchill Livingstone; 1997

Pert C. *The Molecules of Emotion: The Science Behind Mind–Body Medicine.* Simon & Schuster, Inc; 1997;

Natea M, Joosten LAB, Latz E, et al. “Trained immunity: a program of innate immunity memory in health and disease.” *Science* 2016;

Schwartz M, Kipnis J, Rivest S, Prat A. “How do immune cells support and shape the brain in health, disease, and aging?” *J Neurosci* 2013;

Ross CL. “Integral healthcare: the benefits and challenges of integrating complementary and alternative medicine with a conventional healthcare practice.” *Integr Med Insights* 2009;

Tang Y-Y, Hölzel BK, Posner MI. “The neuroscience of mindfulness meditation.” *Nat. Rev. Neurosci.* 2015;

Cahn BR, Delorme A, Polich J. "Occipital gamma activation during vipassana meditation." *Cogn. Process.* 2010;

Kabat-Zinn, J. *Wherever You Go, There You Are: Mindfulness Meditation in Everyday Life.* Hyperion, 1994.

Rubia K. "The neurobiology of meditation and its clinical effectiveness in psychiatric disorders." *Biological Psychology.* 2009;

Astin J.A. "Stress reduction through mindfulness meditation. Effects on psychological symptomatology, sense of control, and spiritual experiences." *Psychotherapy and Psychosomatics.* 1997;

Bishop SR. "What do we really know about mindfulness-based stress reduction?" *Psychosomatic Medicine.* Pubmed; 2002;

Kajimura S, Masuda N, Lau JKL, Murayama K. "Focused attention meditation changes the boundary and configuration of functional networks in the brain." *Sci Rep.* Pubmed; 2020

Barnhofer T., Crane C., Hargus E. "Mindfulness-based cognitive therapy as a treatment for chronic depression." *Behaviour Research and Therapy.* Pubmed; 2009.

Pestonjee D, Pandey S. *Stress and Work: Perspectives on Understanding and Managing Stress.* Sage; 2013.

Carmody J., Reed G., "Mindfulness, spirituality, and health-related symptoms." *Journal of Psychosomatic Research.* Pubmed; 2008;

Popp F, Zhang J. "Mechanism of interaction between electromagnetic fields and living organisms." *Sci China* 2000.

Hunt V. *Infinite Mind: Science of the Human Vibrations of Consciousness.* Malibu Publishing Company; 1996.

Thich Nhat Hanh. *Breathe, You are alive!* Parallax Press; 1987.

Wijk R, Wijk EP. "An introduction to human biophoton emission." *Forsch Komplementarmed Klass Naturheilkd* 2005;

Cohen S, Popp FA. "Biophoton emission of human body." *Indian J Exp Biol* 2003;

Oschman J. *Energy Medicine: The Scientific Basis.* Churchill Livingstone; 2000.

Bassett C. "Fundamental and practical aspects of therapeutic uses of pulsed electromagnetic fields." *Crit Rev Biomed Eng* 1989;

Ross C. "The use of electric, magnetic, and electromagnetic field for directed cell migration and adhesion in regenerative medicine." *Biotechnol Prog* 2017;

Funk R, Monsees T. "Effects of electromagnetic fields on cells: physiological and therapeutic approaches and molecular mechanisms of interaction." *Cells Tissues Organs* 2006;

Funk H, Monsees T, Ozkucur N. "Electromagnetic effects — from cell biology to medicine." *Prog Histochem Cytochem* 2009;

Cohen D, Palti Y, Cuffin BN, Schmid SJ. "Magnetic fields produced by steady currents in the body." *Proc Natl Acad Sci USA* 1980;

Ross C, Harrison BS. "The use of magnetic field for the reduction of inflammation: a review of the history and therapeutic results." *Altern Ther Health Med* 2013;

Tennant J. *We Need a New Medical Paradigm. Healing Is Voltage.* Createspace 2013.

Varga S, Heck DH. "Rhythms of the body, rhythms of the brain: respiration, neural oscillations, and embodied cognition." *Conscious Cogn* 2017;

Becker R. *The Body Electric: Electromagnetism and the Foundation of Life.* William Morrow & Co., Inc; 1985.

Stojilkovic S, Tabak J, Bertram R. "Ion channels and signaling in the pituitary gland." *Endocr Rev* 2010;

Bajpai R, Brizhik L, Del Giudice E, Finelli F, Popp FA, Schlebusch KP. "Light as a trigger and a probe of the internal dynamics of living organisms." *J Acupunct Meridian Stud* 2010;

DeAngelis T. "A bright future for PNI: psychologists' work in the field of psychoneuroimmunology is expanding the understanding of how psychosocial factors can protect or damage our health." *Am Psychol Assoc* 2002.

Jandová A, Pokorný J. "Diseases caused by defects of energy level and loss of coherence in living cells." *Electromagn Biol Med* 2015;

Joshi BC. "Neurology in ancient India." *Indian J Hist Sci.* 1986;

Kunhan Raja C. *Dasopanishadas* (Yoga Kundalini Upanishad) 1935.

Frawley D. "Kundalini and the chakras: Awakening the subtle body." *Yoga and Ayurveda Self Healing and Self-Realization.* Motilal Banarsidass; 2013.

McMurray S. "Chakra talk: Exploring human energy systems." *Holist Nurs Pract.* 2005;

Sanches L, Daniels M. "Kundalini and transpersonal development: Development of a kundalini awakening scale and a comparison between groups." *Transpersonal Psychol Rev.* 2008.

Rubik B. *Scientific analysis of the human aura. Measuring Energy Fields State of the Science.* Backbone Publishing Co; 2004

Prakash S, Chowdhury AR, Gupta A. "Monitoring human health by measuring the biofield 'Aura': An overview." *Int J Appl Eng Res.* 2015.

Albanese CL. "The Aura of Wellness: Subtle Energy Healing." *Relig Am Cult.* 2000.

Lansdowne Z. "Etheric Chakras" *The Chakras and Esoteric Healing.* Weiser Books; 1986.

Klotsche C. *Colour Medicine.* Light Technology Publishing; 1993.

Azeemi, Khawaja Shamsuddin. *Colour Therapy.* Al-Kitab Publications; 1999.

Graham H. *Discover Colour Therapy.* Ulysses Press; 1998.

Pleasanton A. *Blue and Sunlight.* Claxton, Reuser & Haffelfinger; 1876.

Babbitt E. *Principles of Light and Colour.* Kessinger Publishing; 1942.

Ott J. *Health and Light: The Effects of Natural and Artificial Light on Man and Other Living Things.* Devin-Adair Pub; 1972.

Walker M. *Power of Colours.* Avery Publishing Group; 1990.

Daykin N, Joss T. "Arts for health and wellbeing: An evaluation framework." *Public Health England.* 2016.

McClellan R. "The Power Within: The Healing Forces of Music: History, Theory, and Practice." *Lincoln: iUniverse;* 2000.

Sundar S. *Music therapy education: Developmental perspectives. International Perspectives in Music Therapy Education and Training: Adapting to a Changing World.* Charles C Thomas; 2015.

Staricoff R, Clift S. *Arts and music in healthcare: An overview of the medical literature,* 2011.

Dolan P, Testoni S. "Assessing the relationships between engagement in music and subjective wellbeing." 2016.

Baldari C, Macone D, Bonavolontá V, et al. "Effects of music during exercise in different training status." *The Journal of Sports Medicine and Physical Fitness* 2010;

Blood AJ, Zatorre RJ, Bermudez P, Evans AC. "Emotional responses to pleasant and unpleasant music correlate with activity in paralimbic brain regions." *Nat Neurosci.* 1999;

Koelsch S, Kasper E, Sammler D, Schulze K, Gunter T, Friederici AD. "Music, language and meaning: brain signatures of semantic processing." *Nat Neurosci.* 2004.

Platel H, Baron JC, Desgranges B, Bernard F, Eustache F. "Semantic and episodic memory of music are subserved by distinct neural networks." *Neuroimage.* 2003;

Baumgartner T, Lutz K, Schmidt CF, Jäncke L. "The emotional power of music": 2006;

Zatorre RJ, Belin P, Penhune VB. "Structure and function of auditory cortex: music and speech." *Trends Cogn Sci.* 2002;

Suda M, Morimoto K, Obata A, Koizumi H, Maki A. "Emotional responses to music: towards scientific perspectives on music therapy." *Neuroreport.* 2008;

Juslin PN, Sloboda JA, editors. *Music and emotion: Theory and Research* Oxford University Press; 2001.

Huron D. "Is music an evolutionary adaptation?" *Ann N Y Acad Sci.* 2001;

Scherer KR, Zentner MR. "Emotional effects of music" Dept of Psychology, Oxford University Press; 2001.

Balkwill L-L, Thompson WF. "A Cross-Cultural Investigation of the Perception of Emotion in Music: Psychophysical and Cultural Cues." *Music Percept An Interdiscip J.* 1999;

Savage PE, Brown S, Sakai E, Currie TE. "Statistical universals reveal the structures and functions of human music." *Proc Natl Acad Sci U S A.* National Academy of Sciences; 2015;

Becker J. "Exploring the habitus of listening." *Handb Music Emot Theory*, Res Appl. 2010;

Balkwill L. L., Thompson W. F. "A cross-cultural investigation of the perception of emotion in music: Psychophysical and cultural cues." *Music Perception.* 1999;

Bensimon M, Gilboa A. "The impact of the musical presentation on the sense of purpose in life and on self-consciousness." *The Arts in Psychotherapy* 2010;

Burns JL, Labbé E, Arke B, et al. "The effects of different types of music on perceived and physiological measures of stress." *Journal of Music Therapy* 2002;

Koelsch S. "A neuroscientific perspective on music therapy." *Annals of the New York Academy of Sciences.* 2009;

Campion M, Levita L. "Enhancing positive affect and divergent thinking abilities: Play some music and dance." *Journal of Positive Psychology* 2014;

Solé C, Mercadal-Brotons M, Gallego S, et al. "Contributions of music to quality of life." *Journal of Music Therapy* 2010;

Holick MF, Chen TC. "Vitamin D deficiency: a worldwide problem with health consequences." *Am. J. Clin. Nutr.* 2008;

Cashman KD, Dowling KG, "Vitamin D deficiency in Europe: pandemic?" *Am J Clin Nutr.* 2016;

Van Schoor NM, Lips P. "Worldwide vitamin D status. Best Pract." *Res. Clin. Endocrinol. Metab.* 2011;

Kabat Zinn J. *Full Catastrophe Living: Using the Wisdom of your Body and Mind to Face Stress, Pain and Illness.* Bantam Books; 1990;

Prince M., Patel V., Saxena S. *No Health Without Mental Health.* Lancet. 2007.

Ram Dass. Polishing the Mirror: How to Live from Your Spiritual Heart; Love Serve Remember Foundation; Sounds True; 2013.

Made in the USA
Middletown, DE
09 August 2021

45705084R00189